CUSTOMER DRIVEN LEADERSHIP

LEGACY EDITION

DEDICATION

For leaders intent on building a legacy of sustainable success by developing the very best in people, process, and product... profitably. Leaders who are strong enough to trust their vision, their values and their teams of empowered people... teams developed and authorized by them to deliver extraordinary results. Leaders who stimulate innovation, excellence, and esprit de corps... never afraid to measure what matters to ensure their promises to the shareholders, customers, and employees are met to the greatest extent possible.

CONTENTS

Foreword	1
Preface	7
CHAPTER 1 The Transformational Power of Servant Leadership	15
CHAPTER 2 Why Choose the CDL Freedom Formula?	31
CHAPTER 3 Customer Driven Performance Assessment	63
CHAPTER 4 Key Performance Indicators	73
CHAPTER 5 The Geometrics of Customer Driven Leadership	95
CHAPTER 6 Preparing and Assessing for Customer Driven Leadership	117
CHAPTER 7 Customer Driven Leadership Implementation Overview	135
Conclusion	161
Epilogue	169
Glossary	175
Acknowledgements	177
About the Authors	181

FOREWORD

As a young man, I was deeply interested in psychology to understand how and why we humans think, feel, and act as we do…with the intent of helping lift up lives out of fearful, twisted thinking and our joy-robbing, limiting beliefs, and delusions we believe are true. At first, I thought, perhaps I would explore a traditional clinical practice. But I did a clinical residency and quickly realized the constraints of a 30–40-year, one-on-one treatment practice would not likely improve the general human condition to any significant degree. I thought, well, I don't really want to do one-on-one patient work; not when I see all the needs there are in the world. So my work naturally began to expand into helping organizations grow into more authentic, healthier, creative productive forces. I felt that if I could help transform the performance levels, management cultures, and values of influential organizations, the changes would transform the lives of hundreds and then thousands of people. So, I focused my professional graduate training on human learning and development and then my professional efforts in comprehensive organizational development and performance enhancement.

My first major application of that focus occurred when I was invited to become an astronaut training planner and flight crew manager early in the space shuttle program. My task was to take disparate engineering materials and diagrams of the spaceship and payloads and turn them into a shuttle university. Along with a number of other engineering professionals, we pulled together a "de facto" university in the astronaut office and worked with the military and scientific folks one considers to have, "the right stuff," for super-excellent performance under extreme conditions. This opportunity taught me that I have a passion for identifying "the right stuff" and setting up both individual learning opportunities and organizational support to help people reach their maximum performance potential on behalf of worthwhile organizations. I was inspired by the enormous business and social impact.

When the space shuttle Challenger exploded in the 1980s, I watched the analysis of the causes of that disaster. This horrible moment happened as a direct result of top-down, arrogant, decision-making disconnected from the impact on the "paying customer." In this case, the astronaut crew was the customer and they paid for the flawed management decisions with their lives! When management made their decisions to launch the spaceship in untested conditions, these people at the top of the hierarchical organizational chart ignored the warnings and advice of "lower level" frontline aerospace engineering professionals and killed the ultimate customer---which in this case was the space crew itself. I knew the crew. I felt deeply saddened and angry as I watched the harm that a bureaucracy disconnected from the needs of its precious customers can do. It essentially killed people by not having the kind of effective organizational communication structures of shared problem solving, respect for the frontline experts, and putting the customer first. Disgusted and disheartened, I thought, *There has to be a better way here.*

I wanted people to stand up—as individuals and as teams—to create real organizational, substantive change for the good of the organization and the customers. This inspired me to develop a method for ensuring what I thought would be the best practice in management— a passionate engagement on behalf of the customer. Otherwise, why do you exist as an organization? I aimed to weave the best of: process quality control; constant creative problem solving; dedicated, measured customer focus; and authentic positive consequence management into a daily way of life in private and public organizations. In short, I wanted to create great organizations with enjoyable, successful operational cultures.

During that time, I learned a lot about the entrepreneurial mindset; my own and that of world business leaders. In major corporations, it can often be intensely, blindly profit—and power—oriented. However, if you turn that intensity towards customer service data in a servant leadership model—wherein the leaders actually care about their employees and focus on lifting them up to their highest and best selves—everyone's decisions and processes naturally move the organization towards profit goals and customer satisfaction goals. Decisions become intentionally and necessarily both creative and analytical while empowered teams become self-winding toward achievement of their customer service data targets.

The method I designed became known as Customer Driven Leadership (CDL). I began to apply the CDL strategy in Spain and Australia with my mentor Wilson Harrell, entrepreneur extraordinaire (e.g., leader of Formula 409 product success, Publisher of Inc. Magazine and, at the time of our collaboration, a multi-year entrepreneurship advisory columnist in "Success" magazine. Word of mouth began to spin from those organizations. This stuff works! This particular 3-part formula and its healthy habit patterns really do get that organization to become what it intends to be …in a healthy, enjoyable, profitable way. CDL took off throughout the 90s and early 2000s. The organizations which used it got great results.

During the Great Recession of 2008, many organizations experienced an absolute undermining of quality movements which fostered employee involvement and risk taking. Economic challenges ravaged corporations who experienced economic challenges which led to a drastic decrease in employee rights. It was obvious that what was once a national focus on healthy quality-driven, customer-centric cultures died off… and employees lost any sense of rights or power and then any real desire to help lift their greed-centered corporations.

It's now time to bring forth CDL tools again… in this legacy edition. The application of these tools really works. At a time when the world needs these classic tools, we need to dust off this strategic technique and remind people of their potential for creating success… amazing successes. If we can present CDL in terms people can appreciate today, then we have a powerful legacy for all those who have worked in the fields of organizational development. We want to see this movement thrive again.

People have made fortunes using this CDL technique. People's lives have changed for the better; emotionally, spiritually, and financially. People have retired wealthy because their company followed the techniques, allowing them freedom of time and money. It's all possible with sensible applications of the CDL method. It's all proven.

For CDL to be its most powerful, it needs to be implemented with the most authentic concern for the organization, for the people, for their hearts, their minds, and their souls, and collectively, the soul of the company. You must have, or develop rapidly with consultant assistance, a deep understanding of and commitment to employee, corporate, and client well-being. That's foundational. CDL can then harness your experience in understanding how organizations work to lead teams through empowered, confident, data-driven problem-solving, and nurture leaders' ability to bring folks together to uncover and apply unique, market-penetrating, growth-sustaining solutions consistently and rapidly.

This book is not only our legacy but yours. With CDL, you will tap and authorize virtually unlimited human potential to create and sustain a remarkable performance trajectory for your organization by focusing on those who matter most—your customers and employees.

Sincerely,
Dr. Ted Anders

PREFACE

If you have a job description less clear than mine, I'd love to hear about it. If I have to explain it in a vacuum, it often leads to looks of confusion. I have quite a few skills and a subset of those are to mastery-level (I have been called a polymath before). How I best help people starts with who they are and what kind of gaps they have in what they are trying to do. The best way I have figured out how to explain it is that I "catalyze and synergize with the genius of others." I encourage and help people have clarity in how to get from where they are to where they want to be, avoiding pitfalls and unlocking additional opportunities along the way. I also help identify and mitigate gaps, risks, and problems.

My *Unique Ability* (trademark owned by Strategic Coach) is to quickly adapt and build trust, absorb knowledge, discern connections, optimize strategies, overcome problems, and positively influence outcomes in order to maximize success, to protect against risk, to oppose evil and injustice, and to fight for what is right and true.

> "... as we know, there are known knowns; there are things we know we know. We also know there are known unknowns; that is to say we know there are some things we do not know. But there are also unknown unknowns—the ones we don't know we don't know."
>
> **DEFENSE SECRETARY DONALD RUMSFELD, 2002**

That quote from Secretary Rumsfeld sums up a good chunk of what I do. I help people and organizations become aware of the "unknown unknowns" in the things that are important to them and provide strategies on how to positively influence those now "known knowns" and "known unknowns". I see how people and things come together, how they function, how they interact, where things can go wrong, where things can be improved, hidden opportunities, and what lurks in the darkness. The U.S. military in the 1990s coined the term VUCA, for Volatility, Uncertainty, Complexity, and Ambiguity. I am really good at solving for VUCA. One way I help is by asking thought-provoking questions and creating disaster simulations (exercises) that evaluate preparedness. I sometimes describe that as 'I break things for Good'.

I've worked in and for the U.S. military, starting off as an Army paratrooper and Spanish Linguist and ending up as a contract military intelligence instructor and course developer. I ran a top-tier physical security company with over 400 employees in a very volatile part of the world, San Pedro Sula, Honduras. I helped improve Cyber Security in global financial institutes and the U.S. financial services industry. I have also worked with C-suite Executives and many small business owners. I am a certified speaker/trainer/coach with Maxwell Leadership, and I am actively coached, engaged, and growing with Dan Sullivan's Strategic Coach community. I am also a member of a family of 100 global experts called BIP100 (Business is Personal). In my long, rewarding life journey, I've met a lot of fascinating people. One of those people is Dr. Ted D. Anders.

I met Ted at a wedding in Florida while my wife Carolina Batres and I were trying to figure out how we were going to raise money to build a nursing school facility in Central Honduras (my wife and daughter were born in Honduras). Ted and his partner, Dr. Jose Anival Delgado, were looking for a charity to support that was medical, educational, and ideally in Honduras. Turns out that Carolina and Jose were cousins, Jose's family is from Siguatepeque (where the nursing school is), and that Carolina, Ted, and Jose were all going to be there at the same time. We committed to helping the Nightingale Nursing School started by Reverenda Vaike Madisson Molina in 2011 by working on building the team and seeking out great partners to help with funding. Our team was able to raise over $235k from generous partners who shared our vision of making a difference. With the help of Jose's sisters, Victoria Delgado (a brilliant and eco-focused architect, artistic designer, and project manager) and Gracia Delgado-Lavallee (an amazing teacher and coordinator), and many others, we built an ecologically sound modern nursing school with an event center and added a clinic and pharmacy for taking care of the people in the area. Ted's long-time mentor and consulting colleague, Beverly Fisher, was instrumental in obtaining substantial funding to help us get the project "kick started." That's how Ted's teams work together!

Despite having successfully worked hand-in-hand on the school campus development project over a seven-year period, Ted and I only recently had the opportunity to collaborate together within our fields of genius. Ted brought in pieces of three of his proprietary development programs to help forge a partnership with our nursing school team and with the Episcopal Bishops of Honduras, El Salvador, and Guatemala (Bishops Lloyd Allen, David Alvarado, and Silvestre Romero, respectively). I was able to anticipate what Ted was trying to accomplish and helped optimize and ignite the possibilities of what we could do as a united team. With the blessing and support of the bishops, we have formed the LoveLight Campaign for Central America and are committed to building a transformational international team focused on solving root causes of irregular migration and instability in the Northern Triangle Countries leading to increased security and opportunity where people are not only safe, but the countries grow to be amazing places to raise families with new capabilities and solutions to share with other troubled areas of the world.

Dr. Ted Anders is the brilliant organizational psychologist and mastermind behind a revolutionary way of organizing your business so that servant leadership filtered through your vision becomes the predominant culture, and the people are valued and rewarded for solving issues before they become problems.

Preface

In any organization, the primary goal is to always effortlessly exceed customer expectations, even as those expectations are changing, so that you leave the customer wanting to work with no one else in your field. Ted has helped create revolutionarily, successful organizations upon this ideology and is sharing the secrets of his success. He calls this system of organization Customer Driven Leadership, or CDL. He developed CDL in the 1990s and published the first edition of *Customer Driven Leadership: Reviving the Human Spirit for Power and Profit* in 2000. Even though Ted has been semi-retired, CDL is still at work helping massively successful companies and organizations run smoothly with an enriched servant, leadership-led culture, as well as helping them stay ahead of their competition today.

When Ted provided me a deep-dive on CDL, I immediately saw the genius in the formula, which solves for the most difficult aspects of running an organization at peak optimization. Going back briefly to my gifts, I see the flaws and gaps in things, and with CDL what I saw was a self-supported structure of brilliant solutions that solved problems quickly and strengthened every aspect of the organization's focus on success, including the human factors. It is very rare for me to see something so well-designed that can self-correct and self-heal. I pride myself on being able to break anything (for Good), and to be fair, I know where to jam things in the spokes of CDL, but breaking it means not using it as designed. Ted expressed that he would be willing to come out of retirement if I was willing to take the lead as a co-author of CDL with him so that he could share the concepts of CDL on a worldwide scale. I did my due diligence and talked to organizations impacted by CDL over the last 25 years, and their feedback all reinforced my initial assessment of how well CDL was designed. I am excited to share some of that feedback throughout this book through an anonymized lens that protects the privacy of Ted's early adopting clients, many of whom are very successful but discreet entrepreneurial multi-millionaires and billionaires. As you might expect, much of the implementation guidance was provided under strict non-disclosure agreements.

This Legacy edition builds on Ted's original manuscript, with additional real-world and hypothetical examples I have added to help explain some core concepts of CDL. Some of the more technical information we have pulled into a second book called the Customer Driven Leadership Implementation Guidebook that will help with those wishing to self-implement CDL. I have also added interviews with Ted. I want you to hear the concepts explained straight from the creator of CDL. I've also asked a good friend of ours to contribute his personal experiences with implementing and maintaining CDL over the past 25 years, building his company from nine people and a one-million-dollar investment into a vast corporate campus with hundreds of employees generating 10 figure annual revenue. While he chose to remain anonymous, he was thrilled to tell readers how using the key tenets from CDL radically transformed and sustained his organization and those who work there.

This book is intended to share the key concepts of CDL and how it magnifies impact in organizations with a strong vision and positive values. It will show you how collecting and responding to customer feedback, empowering teams to innovate and problem solve, and through becoming a true servant leader will change your organization's culture for the better, create a self-managing organization where people love to work and add value, as well as scale your success beyond your wildest dreams.

I hope the power of CDL synergizes with your vision, values, and genius as well as catalyzes courageous leadership in you and your organization!

Sincerely,
Daniel Hammond

CHAPTER 1
THE TRANSFORMATIONAL POWER OF SERVANT LEADERSHIP

"I started my business in 1994 and it was terribly successful in its first year. The problem was, one day I looked around and realized I had hired a bunch of mercenaries. I never wanted my business to be like that. In the past, I had left a major corporation who bought a good company and I watched that good company get eaten by the machine. I never wanted to be like them and we were headed down that road. Sometimes, you hire mercenaries to get the job done and, after a year, I came to the realization that we were becoming... jerks!

> Then, I bumped into Ted Anders at a school parent gathering and it was just that simple. Dr. Ted spoke to me about CDL and I got to hear what he was experimenting with. I knew this was exactly what I wanted because it didn't sound like Corporate America. Ted was looking for somebody who could implement and validate CDL. I jumped right into it."
>
> **ANONYMOUS CDL ADVOCATE**

Bureaucracy is like a slow-growing cancer, which can suck the life out of an organizational host. It can even cause corporate "death" in an insidious, nearly undetectable manner…until it is too late to save the "patient". Continuing this medical analogy, Ted Anders refers to the symptoms of the "cancers" as "bureausis" – the bureaucratic, neurotic, disabling fear of failure, embarrassment, or negative retribution which builds up in employees and chokes their spiritual vitality… which is the source of innovation, passion, competitiveness, and commitment.

As "bureausis" increases in otherwise healthy, vibrant adults, their natural spiritual light of caring, commitment, creativity, and hope begins to flicker and fade. If an infected organization is to survive, everyone must use powerful medicine to eradicate the spirit-killing cancers of FEAR, GREED, SKEPTICISM, SHORT SIGHTEDNESS, AND GENERAL NEGATIVITY—and related behaviors of butt-kissing, back-stabbing, and gutless lack of accountability.

The "root causes" of unhealthy, unsustainable "deadly" workplace cultures are:

1. Fear among mid-managers because of constant push by senior execs for more profit this quarter… NOW!… without taking into account long-term, sustainability factors;

2. Greed and short-term thinking rampant among executives and boards (including their stock advisors) and;

3. Skepticism, negativity and "buy-out-burn-out" among front-line workers.

The "root causes" can be so prevalent that these three groups (mid-managers, executives and boards, and front-line workers) don't know how to behave when some of their own competent colleagues actually stand up and take a risk to change and improve things. And then, when a few committed competent employees continue to stretch themselves by providing higher quality products, services, and interpersonal relationships, many leaders have a problem giving consistent, meaningful, financial appreciation to keep it going. Meanwhile, "burned-out", nay-saying co-workers can become petty, jealous, and negative.

Unfortunately, the "root causes" of blocked competitive achievement have become accepted as inevitable in many workplaces. For example, just interview employees of the major telecommunication and financial services companies who staff the customer service, call processing, and claims processing centers. They are monitored, recorded on a daily basis and, after such a joyful experience, are often carved up and laid off each time a major buyout occurs.

The most powerful, effective medicine I have encountered to protect an organization against cancerous "bureausis" is a healthy injection of entrepreneurial servant leadership beginning with the HEAD (i.e. senior executives) and spreading systematically throughout the rest of the corporate BODY.

You might be asking, what is "SERVANT LEADERSHIP," or what constitutes a servant leader? Let me share with you my basic, practical understanding. It means leaders lifting up everyone by doing the most "Good" they can for others—so all can achieve their greatest, most satisfying, profitable performance. Servant Leadership occurs when a courageous leader in the established hierarchy is willing to turn things upside down and put the needs of his or her employees and their customers above his or her own. According to world renowned leadership expert John Maxwell in his book *The 21 Irrefutable Laws of Leadership,* he teaches about servant leadership inside his Law of Addition, which states "Leaders add value by serving others." It also goes on to say: "The best place for a leader isn't always the top position. It isn't the most prominent or powerful place. It's the place where he or she can serve the best and add the most value to other people." The beauty of servant leadership is a shared goal and the absolute focus on delivering what is needed so that the end users (customers, clients, larger organization, community) get exactly what they need in the way they need it.

Servant leadership does not mean that the leader gives up authority or accountability to meet the shareholders' expectations or governmental regulation compliance. Rather, within the constraints of such expectations, the leader wholeheartedly serves the needs of his or her employees—so they can, in-turn, serve others who rely on them for a product or service.

The manner with which servant leadership is provided is critical to its success. Typical leadership "services" such as coaching, training, advocacy, resource acquisition, mediation, planning, communication, etc. must be done with patience and a genuine desire to bring out the best in others. However, in today's cutthroat, competitive market, to be true "value adds," these leadership services must be provided for the clear purpose of helping others satisfy the primary expectation of the organization's customers. In organizations fighting for market share, aka competing, there is often a fear to spend time and money to train people because they might leave as they outgrow their current roles, but that mindset will leave your team feeling undervalued and under motivated to serve the rest of the team, including the customers. This is a strategy that positions competitor organizations to take the best employees and customers away—and then there will be no need for employees or leaders!

WHAT IS CUSTOMER DRIVEN LEADERSHIP?

Customer Driven Leadership is an organizational strategy where the "customers" are one's direct employees, members of other departments and, ultimately, the external "paying" customer.

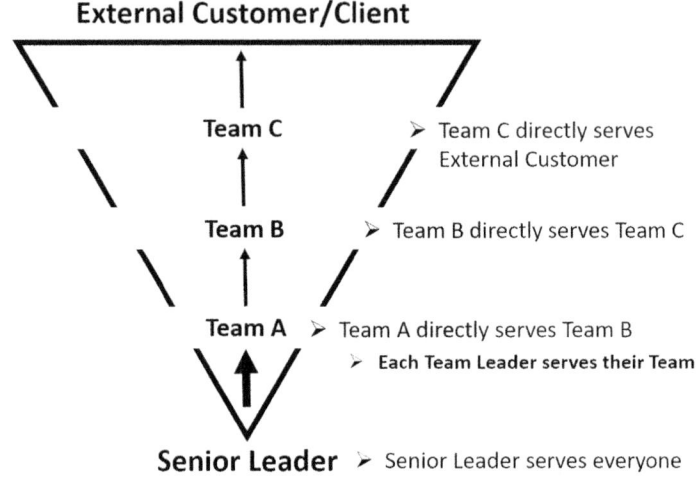

Diagram 1

CDL places the customer at the top of the organization, capturing the power of servant leadership and entrepreneurship to serve internal and external customers in an accountable, caring, and creative manner, which brings spirit and passion alive again!

BBy implementing a 3-part technique which focuses on Customer Driven Performance Assessment, incentives, and high-performance teamwork, your organization will not only increase its level of success, but employees will find themselves with clarity of purpose and expectations. They will become empowered to be successful and to make a difference. They will feel valued and rewarded for their unique contributions to the success of the team. They will enjoy job security and strong potential for growth within a healthy organization, which is essentially what employees want from their jobs, isn't it? The leaders of the organization start by serving more, but as CDL optimizes and people within the organization begin to innovate and work together to solve the day-to-day problems, those leaders begin to experience what Dan Sullivan calls the Four Entrepreneurial Freedoms: Time, Money, Relationship, and Purpose. Since the organization's day-to-day problems are already being solved, those leaders are free to envision, innovate, and solve for what comes next.

CDL has over 25 years of tried, tested, and true experience behind it. Organizations who have adopted CDL declare that their employee retention rate has increased exponentially because the organization has become a family where everybody is valued. Everybody has their part, and everybody is evaluated for what they deliver for the organization. Expectations are clear cut ahead of time, so employees know exactly what is needed to be successful. Everyone's opinion is heard and valued, and there are countless opportunities to be rewarded for innovation.

CDL becomes the skeleton and the circulatory system of your company's identity. It's not a set of rules to manipulate people's behavior. CDL reinforces and expands your values, which becomes the defining feature of who you are. *This is our organization. These are our values. This is what we are working towards. This is how we serve.*

> "CDL became the vision and the strategy at our company. It's like Bruce Lee—it wasn't that he understood Martial Arts; he became Martial Arts. We became our values through CDL."
>
> **ANONYMOUS CDL ADVOCATE**

WHAT CDL ADDRESSES

CDL is the antidote to "bureausis." It is the cure for fear, greed, skepticism, shortsightedness, and negativity. Through the lens of servant leadership, many exciting possibilities rise to the surface.

- Leaders are no longer required to micromanage employees, processes, or their companies.
- Customers provide feedback, telling you explicitly what they want, how they want it, and how well you are delivering it for them.
- Employees gain clarity, purpose, empowerment, and increasing loyalty.
- Self-winding teams are empowered to act within limited authority and run smoothly.
- Teams are able to self-correct and take action to get ahead of problems.

- Innovation is incentivized.
- Data keeps you in close contact with customers and early market trends.
- A strong sense of community emerges, pinpointing where the company fits into the industry, its community(ies) (physical locations), and the world.

In the following chapters, I will break down the components of Customer Driven Leadership, providing insight into the benefits and the implementation process. You'll hear valuable advice from Dr. Ted Anders, as well as success stories from our anonymous advocate. By the end of this book, you will have a good overview and understanding of how CDL empowers organizations with enough information to decide if CDL resonates with how you want to run your organization and serve your clients.

Let's begin.

CONVERSATIONS WITH TED ANDERS

Daniel:
Ted, what is your definition of servant leadership?

Ted:
I think the definition is multifaceted or multi-layered. There is certainly the deep, deep root of it, which is actually a spiritual

rooting. It's one's recognition that the real power of human performance comes when we tap into our understanding of our spiritual power; the fact that we are eternal, divinely expressed, powerful beings. We don't have to be limited beings—limited by self-talk, cultural pressures, or the negative experiences we've had. We are much bigger than that. A leader, an entrepreneurial servant leader, is one who believes this sincerely about humans and wants to have each person attain an increasing experience of their mastery, which comes from the deep nature of who they are, as an expression of Spirit, so to speak.

Then there's the practical logistics of servant leadership, which means we actually have to be willing, as leaders, to flip an organization upside down and place senior leadership ownership at the bottom of a chart. It's about being willing to be the servant who lifts up the organization and willing to place our own ego aside. It means being open to being told we maybe aren't doing something in exactly the way people need it in order to do their job as they understand it or have been assigned. A servant leader has to be open to receive feedback and understand that everything is aimed at the good and well-being of the organization and, ultimately, the customers.

There is a significant difference between that leadership and being a manager.

Daniel:
Absolutely. I think CDL, and correct me if I'm wrong, optimizes how well you serve the people above you in the inverted organization.

Ted:
That's beautiful, Daniel. Yes. We're not talking about spending all your time coaching and fluffing and lifting and playing with ego problems and relationship problems. We're talking about providing such support within the context of an entrepreneurial environment, which means a laser-like, customer-focused approach. We're not going to be dealing with all sorts of issues that do not build the business to revenue-stream growth, profitability, and an excellent reputation in their market.

Daniel:
But that's also got to be what's great about it. I mean, one of the biggest, most important things for an employee is to know what the expectations are. We need to clarify expectations in such a way that employees are going to be optimized for serving. And when stuff happens, as it always does, you've got to be resilient and able to deal with it, to continue moving in the right direction.

Ted:
Exactly, Daniel. I like your reference to resilience because that's really what the servant leader is doing/being. CDL creates the cultural platform on which people build value

about themselves; testing out their own capacities within authorization fields that don't put the organization at risk and having them begin to realize I'm *powerful; of course, I'm a master in my area.* That's one of the things that an inspirational servant leader does. It's, you know, it's not unlike what we hear from stories throughout the history of an inspirational military leader who's willing to go along the lines and say, *Folks, we have this unbelievable challenge. And of course, we're shaking in our boots. Of course, we don't necessarily know what's across the hilltop, but we're as prepared as we can be. We have the resources that are necessary, and with me right here with you, let's go forward together.*

Daniel:
While readers might not be familiar with CDL, they may have heard of the Entrepreneurial Operating System. EOS is an organizational focusing tool and meeting optimization tool, allowing you to go into each meeting with an agenda that says, we're going to cover this, this, this, and this. When that is done, we end the meeting. EOS also helps clients and employees provide input on how valuable the meeting was. The answer should always be 10/10. If not, you need to be figuring out why and what went wrong. It helps the owner or operator evolve things and establish what's next in line. How is CDL different from EOS?

Ted:
Organizations need a self-sustaining, self-winding corporate culture that will actually ensure a specific type of thinking is

measurably occurring and is absolutely tied to the financial and visionary success of the organization. It sounds like EOS is similar to CDL in that the standard operating procedures and commitment to constant quality improvement in a quality environment are desirable outcomes.

The problem is, when optimizing business management systems were originally introduced, (such as Total Quality Management, Six Sigma, and ISO) most cultures were still top-down, power-hungry, butt-kissing, money-focused cultures. There was and still is a real hierarchical approach to excellence and quality and process control. And team building around process control didn't necessarily become a real heart-based, core culture that people really felt comfortable with and valued because they weren't really reinforced for that set of behaviors. They were reinforced for what I like to call *The Three Killer B's:* butt-kissing, backstabbing, and "bureausis" for bottom-line money targets.

EOS sounds very much like a very useful, accurate set of tools that can keep companies focused on their brighter future. When we begin to discuss the "Geometrics of CDL," we will show how that aspect of CDL supports the empowerment and spiritual dimensions, which will create a next-level culture that can accomplish incredible, healthy growth and virtually eliminate competition through unmatched products and services.

Daniel:
It sounds like EOS starts in a very similar way to CDL. You've got to have a vision. You've got to know where you're going, and you have to have some values to build a culture. Do you see EOS and CDL as complementary and really multiplicative of each other?

Ted:
I think EOS fits right into the heart of the "Geometrics of CDL." Where we have the circle (or a heart symbol) in the center, you could put EOS right in the middle of that because it does boil down to that kind of commitment to cooperatively move the rocks and blocks which have to be moved out of the organization's path. And how are we moving them? You need powerful teams with an agenda and teaming tools to actually make those things happen. So, it's part of the heartbeat of an entire system, but it's not the entire system.

Daniel:
My next question is how can CDL transform how an organization does business?

Ted:
Over decades of applications in a variety of organizations, we've seen a fairly predictable, four-quarter, desirable curve of process, efficiency, revenue, and profitability improvements.

In the first quarter, everyone needs to recognize key processes and relationships are essential to meeting our promise to the external customer so that the organization can grow. In short, folks start to realize inside the organization, *We're all beginning to talk about, focus on, and get control of these processes and key relationships.*

In the second quarter, certainly by the fifth or sixth month, the paying customer, the external folks with expectations of that organization, begin to notice some things improving. For example, for an organization that's delivering a product, their measures might be, "the right product, at the right place, at the right time." Let's say these three easy measures are what a client would expect. They start to notice improvement in those numbers. And of course, through CDL they are giving monthly feedback data, which lets the organization providers know, *oh, they really care about that, and they appreciate it.* So, it starts to become a real, healthy set of communications and improvements.

By the third quarter, you'll begin to see an increase in those scores and a noticeable increase in revenue or other success metrics. Customers are realizing and sharing with others that, *Oh, this organization's better!* Word of mouth starts to spread, expanding the organization's influence and success in the market.

By the fourth quarter, you begin to see that the overall set of corporate health measures, customer satisfaction scores, internal efficiencies, inventory levels, productivity measures, begin to strengthen, and that's sort of the four-quarter set of upward curves that occur. All of this will tell you the new organizational culture-focus is gaining traction.

Daniel:
It's kind of a combination of what you measure is what matters. Because you're capturing the things that are important and increasing awareness all around, right? As you grow CDL within the organization, you're also learning. You start thinking more than just, *I'm pushing my cog forward.* Teams start to work together considering, *how can we optimize every aspect of how our team processes the cogs?* And the organization functions more as if it were a healthy body?

Ted:
I love that you used the term "body". The new or improved culture really becomes what we often wish for in an organization—esprit de corps, the spirit of the body. Understanding that we're serving each other throughout the entire organization, in the inverted organizational chart, from the leadership at the "bottom", all the way up to the external customers. And yes, it brings that set of relationships and expectations of serving one another to life.

CHAPTER 2
WHY CHOOSE THE CDL FREEDOM FORMULA?

As the leader of your organization, you know that customers are at the heart of what you do; therefore, their feedback should be a top-priority because, as it is often said, "No customers, no business."

In Chapter 1 we established that CDL has the power to change your workplace culture from cut-throat, fearful, and competitive to collaborative, proactive, and creative. Creativity and innovation are key to staying one step ahead of the competition and scaling your business with lightning-fast results.

Adults (and kids, for that matter) are at their creative best when "fear" of rejection or negative reprisals is absent, so the

CDL approach is intentionally designed to reduce threatening actions or words by those who have "control" over others.

Specifically, when top leaders are willing to have their employees rate their leadership services and when a significant portion of the boss's bonus compensation is tied to the evaluation, employees' dormant entrepreneurial spirits begin to wake up from years of suppression and bureaucratic captivity. This is especially true when a leader who receives low performance scores doesn't lash out at employees with negative reprisals. If the leader is willing to change and learn new ways to lead and serve, employees' entrepreneurial spirits actually "sit up" and rub the sleep out of their eyes! The thought is, *Hmm, I might actually have a shot at sharing an idea to really make this place come alive! I might actually want to invest my emotions and hopes in this organization.*

On the other hand, the moment a leader punishes a group of employees from which low satisfaction scores emerged, they retreat back to thinking, *Why should we care? It is not our problem, and the boss only cares what we do when complaining about us not doing it to their satisfaction.* That is a tough trend to reverse.

However, if leadership involvement is sincere and incentives are meaningful, CDL begins to produce the following three transformations within just two to six months. First, employees begin to realize that their own futures, just like their boss's, depend on receiving high internal and external customer scores. Next, they begin to make healthy, cooperative, improved decisions within their zones of control – and the magic of entrepreneurial activity has begun! As John Maxwell says in the introduction to his program *Beyond Success,* "In my five decades of working with people and striving to add value to them, I've come to believe that deep down, everyone wants to be successful, live a life of purpose, and make a difference." Finally, capable, talented, creative adults begin to experience the old, ice-cold fears melting under the hot spotlight of fact-based, monthly, Customer Driven Performance Assessment.

To help this emerging entrepreneurial spirit of human freedoms take hold, we introduce a monthly cycle of business process review based on the most recent customer scores. This cycle involves regularly collecting and summarizing scores, such as on the 28th or next business day of each month. This activity should never be allowed to take more than a total of two to three hours per team—or people don't want to do it! In order to ensure that scoring is easy and readily includes external customers around the globe, it is helpful to use web-based tools (like we have at customerdrivenleadership.co) to enable quick, easy scoring, and collection at the end of each month.

During the first week of the new month, departments/teams meet for a standard 45–60 minute agenda to respond to low scores with change actions, which might elevate the scores. Monthly incentives, based on scores from the preceding month, are distributed or reported during the meeting. After the first few months, this cycle becomes the spring of a "self-winding", voluntary corporate mechanism in which employees act like entrepreneurial owners of their processes and customer relationships. Whatever needs to be fixed in order to satisfy the customer gets fixed in a matter of just a few months, at most, because once CDL becomes part of the culture, employees will proactively solve potential problems within their assigned areas. Remember, the leaders are supporting the employees as they make these improvement decisions because the leaders' jobs are to provide leadership in the form of coaching support, not to constantly override or micromanage employees' valid initiatives. Leader overrides would be appropriate only when the employees' initiatives fall outside previously stated limitations, which form "the chalk lines" on the organization's "Playing Field."

Once this cycle of entrepreneurial, service-oriented business change is underway, your organization begins to experience the following vital shifts:

1. Staff, middle managers, and senior leaders are emulating a healthier servant leadership style, while remaining focused on their customers!

2. The sales targets, operations budget, and quality plans become a reality through monthly, self-winding, continuous improvement of processes.

3. Innovation and a sense of personal ownership and commitment emerges among all levels of staff.

4. If the strategic plan has been built on penetrating new customer markets, market access will be activated in measurable ways—monthly!

5. The HR Plan—CDL simplifies and "automates" performance monitoring and incentive plans.

6. Organizational Culture—CDL leads to an entrepreneurial spirit running on incentives earned for customer satisfaction results. There is a strong sense of process ownership among staff. Bureaucratic slow response is greatly reduced—even eliminated!

7. All of this together leaves team members feeling clear on their responsibilities, rewarded for solving problems and improving processes, and valued for how they serve the customer and the organization, all of which reduces turnover.

These seven results constitute a great competitive advantage. When you combine CDL with a business with competitive products or services and a laser-focused marketing plan, the CDL technique will help you realize your maximum operational potential. CDL similarly helps non-profit based organizations better serve their customers or deliver on their objectives.

The success of CDL in your organization depends on breathing new life, a passionate vision, and a genuine sense of "ownership" into employees. The CDL equation is designed to continually invigorate workers who may have been feeling controlled, intellectually and financially "imprisoned", disconnected, underappreciated, or unsure if they even have a future with the organization. The cultures generated by the fears of "down-sizing," "right-sizing", buy-outs, market instabilities, global pandemics, leveraged acquisitions, or other actions that generate workforce instability have led to what is referred to as "Survivors Syndrome".

People stuck in "Survivors Syndrome" become depressed, stressed out, passive-aggressive in their relationships, and much less productive. Many survivors will even sabotage the improvement efforts their struggling organizations are trying to make to gain new levels of productivity and quality. Their level of trust and loyalty is at a lifetime low point, and many traditional efforts to regain it do not deliver results.

LOWER PRODUCTIVITY

Guess what? Based on Ted's research and first-hand experience, the majority of the organizations who take advantage of their employees with short-sighted, manipulative approaches end up with lower productivity than they had before the changes!

Consider this scenario: Leadership thinks the organization is not where it needs to be, so they come up with the following solution: *If each employee can just increase their productivity by 10%, we can make our company goals.* Now consider three employees on a sales team, Andy does 50% of the sales for the team, Barbara does 33%, and Charlie does 17%. Andy is a go-getter—100% focused on his job, and he does his best focusing on sales every single day. Barbara is good at sales, but she also is someone that uplifts the team and helps them feel connected, valued, and optimistically focused. Charlie is the de facto in-house Information Technology (IT) support for not only his team, but six other teams. Charlie isn't excited about sales and looks for opportunities to do other things outside his sales responsibilities.

What happens if we JUST ask for another 10% of sales from each of them? Andy is already going above and beyond and the message he hears is, *You aren't working hard enough,* even though he is already doing half of the sales. Barbara is a team player, so she digs in and spends more time working sales and less time connecting and valuing others, so morale in the organization overall decreases. Charlie now hates sales and doesn't have time to work where his passions are, and when there are IT problems, the rest of the organization now spends 60+ minutes on hold with external IT support instead of having Charlie solve the problem. Charlie and Andy are looking for new jobs, and when they leave, Barbara will leave.

When you combine stress at work with complicated family dynamics, incomplete community support systems, and highly diverse workforces which, if not celebrated and valued, can cause distance between employees, the result is a workforce which isn't always focused on the customer or the competition. You get staff members who are just struggling to stay motivated enough to show up to justify receiving their paychecks. At best, relationships between co-workers and between superiors and subordinates are cordial, and at worst, they can even grow antagonistic and begin to see others in the organization as standing in the way of their success, which can, in turn, lead to hostility, credit stealing, and even political back-stabbing.

THREE FREEDOMS OF A HEALTHY WORKFORCE

In the midst of this mess, we call the workplace, an employee might be able to spend a few hours a day when he or she can actually focus on trying to do a good job and experience the joy that comes with being a mature, capable, creative adult. Nearly all workers want to do a good job but have forgotten or never experienced the Three Freedoms of a Healthy Workforce that form the basis of being able to do a good job every time. These Three Freedoms can help you unshackle the boundless energy of the human spirit which can, in turn, create a leading-edge organization that is almost impossible to beat. In fact, these three freedoms are the driving force behind entrepreneurship, passion, and hope!

The Three Freedoms of a Healthy Workforce are:

- Freedom from threat (inside the organization) and from over control
- Freedom to create
- Freedom to act on creativity

Each of these freedoms must pervade the workplace at all levels. If workers have even the slightest doubt about the reality of these freedoms, they will not take the social and career risks associated with continuous improvement of their performance. They certainly won't display leading edge, creative thought and activity that might rock the boat of convention and business as usual. Finally, they won't develop mutual trust with their coworkers, so the risk-taking (emotional and practical) required for change won't occur.

As a result, your organization will be stuck competing with other organizations that do what you do, instead of forging a path of innovation that elevates the organization above the competition.

OK, just what are these freedoms, and what do they mean in a very practical sense in the day-to-day workplace? These freedoms are worth exploring further because they revive the human spirit and bring out the best in each person. Let's take a look.

FREEDOM FROM THREAT AND OVER-CONTROL

To begin with, let's review Webster's basic definition of *freedom*. It is "the absence of coercion or constraint in choice or action. Also, the liberation from slavery or restraint or from the power of another; independence." As my mentor and global leadership expert John Maxwell says, "Be willing to absorb some risk and failures to allow people freedom to express themselves."

EMPLOYEES ARE STRESSED OUT

Most of the groups we have worked with are stressed out over the fear of manipulative performance reviews, the threat of job loss, and the threat of embarrassment due to failure. They express feeling threatened by co-workers and bosses who are just waiting for them to make a mistake in order to point it out and use it against them. These ever-present threats are used as invisible control devices on the minds and hearts of the workforce. In short, they cause a pervasive handicap in the ranks, which is more expensive to an organization than any other overhead cost component. Threats and control are far too rampant.

As Ted has traveled throughout the United States and around the world, he has seen this threatening manipulation and insidious crippling control, even in major organizations which have spent millions of dollars training everyone on standards like Total Quality Management and other similar systems that should, in theory, increase productivity. In fact, some of the most sophisticated threats and over control can be seen in companies and government agencies that claim to have quality improving systems in place, but really only pay lip-service to some of the world's most successful improvement philosophies.

Example 1

For example, Ted experienced a plant manager in a major assembly facility of a large corporation who continued to curse and scream at his production line supervisors and staff when they pointed out a flaw in the production line process, or dared to insist that a weld be re-done before passing the work down the line. While this is the daily ulcer-producing reality for workers in this plant and around the world, often the same corporations are spending millions on advertising and training programs that "add value" to employees, but are those advertised commitments to quality and pledges to value their workforce really being lived out? Will the corporation actually be delivering something uniquely noticeable to their customers?

Of course, there have been improvements in industries, but there are tens of thousands of employee casualties strewn across the battlefield, and how many industries have decided to offshore labor to pay less and care less about their workforces? We're not just talking about the supposedly "obsolete" workers seen as "dead weight" in a rapidly changing technological work environment. I'm talking about the people still working in the industry, and other industry categories, who are still working but enduring on a daily basis threats and over control of their thoughts and actions.

Example 2

A CDL client, a very successful, well educated CEO of a computer hardware and software firm tells of his experience as an employee of a globe-spanning, high-technology, manufacturing firm. Our client was the head of a 40-person design group in a division which produced performance control hardware for industrial applications. He and his group produced creative designs targeted to specific market niches. When he dared to suggest to his bosses a better way to market the products in these niches, he was told, "You are the arms and legs of this company. We're the head. We'll decide which strategies to use to direct the company. You need to return to your work group and stay focused on your assignments." Only months later, this disgruntled employee became the head of his own company, and in less than a year (using the very strategies he had suggested to his former employer) had sold millions of dollars worth of equipment and software to the markets his former employer previously dominated.

The moral of this story? Don't try to threaten and over control any employee—certainly not the ones who are willing to express creativity and initiative, which could become the engine of a "self-winding" mechanism for growth and improvement in your own company! In fact, it was this very experience which led our client to leave his position and create his own company.

We all know stories like those just related, and we have heard them for years. Quite frankly, at first Ted didn't really appreciate just how devastating workplace threat and control are to the individual and team spirit of freedom and initiative—that critical sense that *I'm worth something, by God, and so are my colleagues!* His recognition of the devastation grew as he worked year after year in all types of organizations and saw and heard the same symptoms crippling human expression and performance. Why do you think W. Edwards Deming, the "father" of the modern business quality movement, in his book Out of the Crisis said, "Eliminate annual performance reviews."? Because the reviews can very easily be used as devices to control and threaten any employee who might dare to speak out, or they can become toothless, useless documents when a supervisor rates everyone high on the job criteria just to keep people from complaining and moaning about who got what score and who likes whom the most.

REMOVE THREATS

We must remove attitudes, behaviors, policies, and procedures that threaten the adult's sense of worth and his or her comfort with sharing ideas that could lead to improved relationships and corporate performance. This is the responsibility of everyone in the organization, and it starts with and remains with the most senior leader and the executive team as they lead, model, and coach with more positive words and actions. Investing in coaching and developing a more inclusive culture can be valuable, but if they do not start at the top, then it is not a truly inclusive and organizational value; is it? How many employees have had some sort of leadership training only to think, *If only my boss understood these values,* and *why am I here? My leadership doesn't care about this stuff.*

Free your employees' spirits from internal, political threats and watch them begin to shine! Yes, you'll have to be sure that all that energy and enthusiasm gets channeled in an appropriate direction, which can help the organization fulfill its vision and strategic objectives. Be the leader your employees need you to be. Go through the training and coaching first and then model what you learn to show your employees that self-improvement matters, and the organization's values matter. And then you will find that the work environment becomes a more enjoyable and prosperous place once you have eliminated the historical need to constantly prod, poke, and threaten employees just to get a temporary level of acceptable performance.

FREEDOM TO CREATE

It is a very rare person that has zero capacity to be creative. The problem is, our public, parochial, and many other private schools have traditionally suppressed creative thought. Remember all those times you were told to "Stop daydreaming and complete your worksheet!" How sad when you consider that daydreaming is related to being able to envision something beyond the daily grind—something beyond "business as usual". Think about it. You or your organization spend lots of money trying to create a vision that will guarantee future success. In many cases, that valuable vision (and the ability to implement it) is only a few inches away from you in the head of one of your employees or co-workers! How do you encourage people to share even "dumb" ideas that might be half of the solution or a new way to look at a problem?

HOW CREATIVITY IS SUPPRESSED

After elementary and secondary school gets finished with us, large corporations, the civil service, or the military hire you and say, *Think and act this way*. After a few more years of having your creativity suppressed, most adults no longer believe they are creative or even remember what it's like. The expression of original, creative thought is the single greatest contributor to America's past economic prowess. In fact, the entrepreneurial, problem-solving spirit is still the single greatest global resource—and it is not depleted! Suppressed, over-controlled, threatened, and nearly strangled to death, in some places, but not depleted. Let's take a deeper look at this thing called "Creativity."

COMPONENTS OF CREATIVE THOUGHT

Creative thought is made of four types of thought:

- Original Thinking
- Flexible Thinking
- Fluent Thinking
- Elaborative Thinking

Any one or all four of these together constitute creative thinking. They are even more powerful when a team comes together and uses these creative thinking types collaboratively to innovate and problem-solve. Here's what we mean by each of these terms.

Original Thinking

Original thinking means generating a new or rare thought. The term innovation is related to this concept. The "nova" part of "inNOVAtion" means "new".

Flexible Thinking

Flexible thinking means being able to see an issue from many different perspectives—from the customer's, worker's or supplier's point of view, from either a macro or micro perspective, from one paradigm or belief system versus another, etc.

Fluent Thinking

Fluent thinking simply means being able to generate a lot of ideas—either a great number of options, solutions, problems, causes, etc.

Elaborative Thinking

Elaborative thinking means adding details, rich, clear imagery, or "fleshing" out the skeletal idea. Elaborative thinking is especially useful when combined with an exciting, innovative, original idea that needs further detail to be meaningful to all parties concerned.

FREE UP CREATIVE TALENTS

If you really want to grow an organization, spend some of your time and money repairing the damage our schools and past management methods have done. We need to focus on freeing the creative talents which are locked inside your employees. Remove the perceived or actual threat that stops employees from trying out a new idea or method. Allow a few mistakes (with calculated risk), and let people gain new skills and confidence by "testing their wings" of creativity. It will pay great dividends in the future.

FREEDOM TO ACT ON CREATIVITY

In order to act on a good idea, you must first remove the threat of negative consequences that employees believe will result from less than perfect attempts to improve their process, product, or service. Then, train and reward creative thought. Third, support improvement actions based on creativity. Of course, their actions must be analyzed and well planned by individuals or teams of employees. This can be done by synergizing with the creative thought processes of other team members. I might have a great idea, but if I cannot see the way to implement it, I might just let it die in my head. If there was a safe way for me to share my idea with the team, someone else might see an easy way to implement it.

LOSS OF DOLLARS

Employees often know exactly how to improve things in the workplace but won't act on the knowledge. This timid, fearful lack of action can cost an organization untold benefits and profits. Imagine if the great idea above was a 5% increase in efficiency or a 5% reduction in cost. What would that mean to the organization?

LOSS OF PRIDE

While the lack of employee action costs money, it also costs the workers their sense of pride and self-worth. Their positive spirit is diminished, and a vicious cycle of threats and temporary responses to threats takes root in the organization. This is the downward spiral from which many companies never recover. It can be a "dead-leaf" spin. Imagine that great idea above. What if I worked up the courage to share that with my boss, and he also could not see a way to implement it and so just said, "I don't see how that could work." How many more ideas will get shared?

ENCOURAGING PROACTIVE ACTIONS

How do you get employees to generate proactive actions on a regular basis? Form Customer Driven Leadership teams in which co-workers can support each other's individual and group improvement efforts. Remove real and perceived threats associated with change and imperfect improvement attempts. Encourage creative, innovative, bold thinking combined with analysis and planning. Then, support actions chosen by the workers who know most about the process, product, or customer affected by the action. These changes in your organization will revitalize the "Esprit de Corps"—the spirit of the corporate body—individually and collectively. This is what your workforce needs!

THE CDL FREEDOM FORMULA

That all sounds great, doesn't it? The question is, how do you do it? The answer lies in three simple steps:

1. **CUSTOMER DRIVEN PERFORMANCE ASSESSMENT** (on a monthly basis):

This approach puts the customer (external and internal) on top of the organization chart. That's why Ted represents CDL with the inverted organization chart symbol, which you saw in the previous chapter:

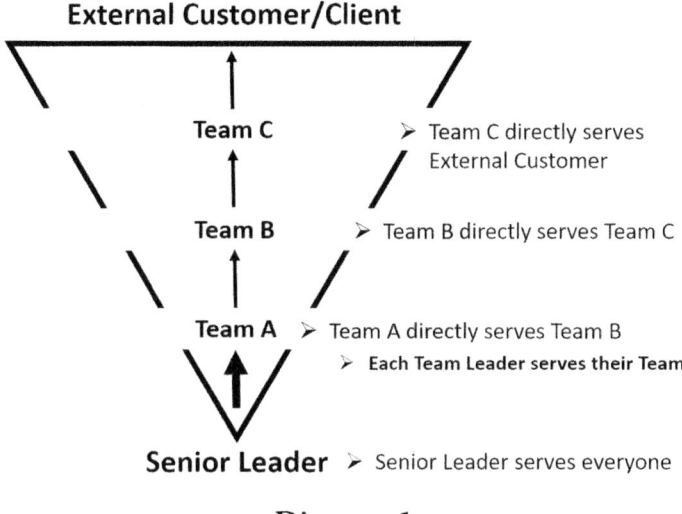

Diagram 1

Then, Ted overlays the Value Chain (i.e. the macro, supply chain process) into the upside down pyramid and has everyone aim their work processes straight at the customer. Customer Satisfaction Assessment flows from the top down. Service and support flow along the Value Chain from the bottom up.

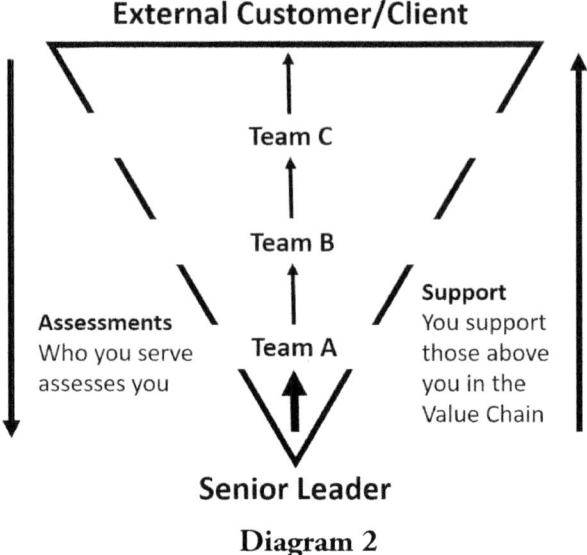

Diagram 2

The CDL Customer Driven Performance Assessment approach supersedes 360-degree feedback if you really want to beat the competition. Although the 360-degree approach can provide valuable insight, it is often just used as a "safe", bureaucratic assessment system. To really break up an expensive, dead-weight bureaucracy, free up entrepreneurial innovation and sponsor servant leadership. It takes Customer Driven Performance Assessment all along the Value Chain… from the inverted top to bottom.

2. **INCENTIVES**

Incentives for entrepreneurial customer focus must be available every 30 days. These "share-the-wealth" payouts (both cash and non-cash) are based heavily on the Customer Driven Performance Assessment scores…with a smaller weighting based on the organization's financial Key Performance Indicators (KPIs). This proportional weighting of incentives is justified by the fact that KPIs are the result of how well customers are served…not the other way around! There are so many ways to provide incentives. What is critical is that it is something significant to the employee, and it should grow as they grow in the organization. Scoring 10 out of 10 should be a rare metric to hit at first, but employees get there by improving the areas of their responsibilities and those of their team.

3. **HIGH PERFORMANCE TEAMWORK**

Teamwork should be focused on Value Chain service improvements. The improvements come from using a process-oriented approach to operations, coupled with the use of Continuous Process Improvement (CPI) tools. In order to improve service to the customer and the organization shareholders, each team must understand its place in the Value Chain and how the team serves other parts of the organization-wide chain. These relationships become the most important internal supplier/customer relationships.

RESULTS OF THE 3-PART FORMULA

When applied according to the guidelines and advice offered throughout this book, the simple 3-part technique leads to:

- A measurable expression of the entrepreneurial spirit (in both customer satisfaction and financial terms)
- Rapid work process improvements
- Much better interpersonal relationships through servant leadership
- More wealth from increased customer purchases and process improvements
- And what's more, the monthly improvement scores connect you at every level with the customers you serve, which are not only great promotional tools for the marketing and sales departments, but also act as radar for shifting market trends that put you ahead of the competition.

THE CORE CONCEPT OF CDL

In order to bring Servant Leadership and a strong Customer Driven, Entrepreneurial culture to life, while wiping out "bureausis", you have to change the entire mindset about who is at the top and bottom of the organizational chart. The concept of inverting the organizational chart has been discussed for decades during the Quality Management era. In most cases, Ted has only seen "lip-service" done to this idea of valuing the employee and customer—putting the employee at the top of the chart just underneath the paying customer.

In CDL, you put the External Customers at the top of the organizational chart. On the next level down, you put the front-line staff of the internal departments who serve them.

The next level includes the supervisors of these "front line" employees. After all, the employees are their supervisor's most important customers. And, as our anonymous client says, "they're billion-dollar assets." This client's organization has used the CDL culture for more than 25 years now and attributes their sustainable, enjoyable, massive growth to the CDL Formula, combined with his original marketing formula and low-price/high-value business model. Below these supervisors come the departments who represent the functions that support the Value Chain, and so forth, all the way down to the CEO and the Board.

In a CDL entrepreneurial, servant-leadership environment, the primary direction of performance assessment is from the paying customer down the Value Chain to the CEO. The primary direction of support and service is the reverse—from the CEO at the bottom to the front-line employees at the top. After all, the front-line staff is closest to the product or service outcomes, which Ted identifies in CDL as "Customer Careabouts."

You might be thinking *Yeah, yeah, yeah, I've heard all that before, but nothing really changes.* Not so with CDL. Every month, every department and leader receives ratings from the level above them on just the three to five most important "Customer Careabouts." For departments or teams, the source of the grades, as well as the grades themselves, are posted on the wall, internal web pages, or sent out via email for everyone to see. Not for the purpose of embarrassing anyone. The purpose is to create a public discussion forum for constructive improvement meetings.

For individuals, all sources of feedback are anonymous, but the scores are still posted for all to see. The monthly ratings are summarized on charts called Customer Driven Performance Team Assessment Chart, Key Performance Indicator Driven Team Assessment Chart, Employee Driven Performance Leadership Assessment Chart (Leadership Assessment), and Employee Driven Performance Teammate Assessment Charts or Customer Driven Performance Employee Assessment Chart (Contributor Assessments). These charts become the DRIVERS of individual and team/department performance improvement.

In order to ensure a constant focus on your customers, the rating from the level above you, on the inverted Value Chain/organization chart, always counts for at least 70% of your monthly performance review. When this technique becomes a reality, it makes "butt-kissing" obsolete. Your boss may like you personally, but if your individual and/or team scores are consistently low, you have a problem. Furthermore, if your boss is getting low-service scores, then that means he or she has a problem meeting their customers' needs—those of the employees! This person is not demonstrating measurable, entrepreneurial, servant leadership!

Think about it. The boss's most important customers should be the employees. If an organization wants front-line staff to get high scores from the external customer or other internal departments, then supervisors and managers must be willing to provide a solid set of leadership services to their employees. Specifically, leaders need to be willing to coach, provide technical guidance, advocate for the team through political storms, and acquire resources and approvals necessary to achieve Customer Careabouts. Hiring, coaching, improvement and growth training, and taking assessments as a team, such as DISC, Koble, and StrengthsFinder, can help the team work better together. At every level, you've got to satisfy the customers in order to have a winning team that can beat your competition.

At this point, you might be saying, *That sounds amazing, but it seems like a lot of work*!

In truth, if you are planning to do a full implementation of CDL, it's going to shake up your organization. You need to consider the Return on Investment (ROI) and think about how quickly you can reap the benefits. We routinely see massive change in three to six months! The incredible thing about CDL is that it is a constantly self-correcting formula. Wherever your customers go, wherever your employees go, whatever is happening in your organization and your industry, it's all highlighted very quickly.

If you want to see substantial growth, you get what you put in. Cultural overhaul is no easy task, but with hard work and dedication, you'll be able to serve your customers with excellence and capture new markets. Because we believe strongly that CDL changes everything, we want you to feel confident in implementing the system. For this reason, in the following pages, we will break down the steps of CDL into tangible, bite-sized pieces. Maybe you only take one piece at a time. Maybe you subscribe to the full-meal deal. Either way, you are working toward success.

> "CDL is the kernel of our operating system. It's how we govern the behavior of our team members. Everything is clearly outlined. CDL is a way to free you up to get quality and results. What it does is create self-winding team members who govern themselves based upon our core values:
>
> 1. Vision—This is where we're going.
> 2. Our Promise / Strategy - How we're going to serve our customer. And one of the biggest elements in serving our customers is that best customer experience.
> 3. Value Chain—The departments of your organization and how they work together to serve and deliver our Promise for our Customers according to our Vision.
> 4. Customer Driven Leadership—The mechanism of empowerment and accountability.

My favorite outcome is that my company has almost zero voluntary turnover. That's a result of two things. One is our CDL hiring practices (finding the right people for the right roles). Two, when people see these constructs and understand what they do and how it all works for the company's success as well as their success, they are totally on board.

Every Tuesday, we have really powerful company meetings because we have each team presenting what they're doing to get us to our Vision 2030 goals of this shiny company on the hill.

I am able to study the public numbers of the four biggest players in our industry. From those numbers, I can see that in sales, per person, we're at least four times more efficient and earn four times as much profit per person. That is a result of CDL. Getting people to understand that we are like a business laser; we're all on the same wavelength is key, but you have to have the vision. You have to have the strategy, and you have to have the Value Chain mapped out. Then you work at it."

ANONYMOUS CDL ADVOCATE

CONVERSATIONS WITH TED ANDERS

Daniel:
How does implementing CDL affect an organization's culture?

Ted:
To many cultures, especially in the modern Western world, we have been ravaged by a couple of years of a pandemic, as well as decades of undermining employees; resulting in a lack of professional security, safety and longevity. In these

tenuous cultures, people don't really deeply commit to their sensitive souls and spiritual side. They are probably thinking, *I've got a lot of power, but it's also very sensitive, and tender, and I don't really want it bashed and bruised.* People kind of hold back. They're always looking at their next best option. There's never that fullness of commitment, and that fullness of commitment often includes the application of one's inherent, amazing, brilliant creativity, and a little bit more risk taking to make breakthroughs for the organization. In tenuous, negative cultures, people are not fully present and fully applying themselves as a general statement.

What happens is when the organization culture becomes CDL, after several months a clear, safe, and stable platform emerges where we gather around the facts that matter. We gather around the intention to lift each other up. We do not allow negative bashing of others around low scores or something that's not moving quite fast enough. We truly do serve to lift each other up. That service looks like coaching, training, resource allocation, very supportive conversations, and some HR intervention, if necessary. We want to support struggling employees so that person and their team can really begin to contribute according to the way the measures require.

CDL essentially helps an organization move away from tenuous, self-oriented cultures to comfortable, safe, creative, productive ones.

Daniel:
You had a subtitle on the first edition of Customer Driven Leadership that was *Reviving the Human Spirit for Power and Profit*. That's kind of an unusual combination of concepts. What does that mean to you and why was it important enough to put in the title?

Ted:
People in less than healthy work cultures hold back one way or another. Therefore, while the organization may be saying to them: *You have the power to make a change. You have the power to be creative. You have the power to fix things, but if you make a big mistake in a meeting or alienate your manager, you pay a high price.*

Basically, what we used to do in these first initial applications of CDL is I would go around a corporation when we were just beginning, and I would put little signs all over the floors and on the walls. *Here's some power. Pick it up!* And we would actually see who would actually own that. The point was, we would then have conversations about the fact that there's power here in this culture.

I think we had some healthy corporate environments for about 20 years in the 1990s and up until 2008. Then, with the ravaging of our economy and the collapse of corporations and so forth, up till now, workers have been at risk. Many companies have just told them, *If you don't like it, get out.*

Our CDL culture is empowering when it comes to people really feeling safe and secure. I think that there's so much power in humans, so much power that leaders would like their people to take, as long as it stays within the authority Playing Field. Within those lines of authority, use your power. Use your creativity.

The original subtitle and CDL culture are about reviving the human spirit. I used to say, *for power, and profit,* but what I would say now is *reviving the human spirit with power for profit.* I would refer to it that way. People are like, *Okay, yes. Yes, I will use my power.* First of all, it's very meaningful to bring your full self to what you do. But then it's also for profit. In the CDL environment, additional profit is shared, proportionally, based on one's ability and willingness to make improvements. So if somebody else gets rich, they are sharing their power because we all gain more.

Daniel:
There are so many people who just have a job they're hanging on to because it pays their bills. Maybe some of them do the minimum, just to not get fired, but as the market shifts, suddenly the corporation needs more productivity from that person, and that person doesn't want to give more productivity. So now the corporation has a great need, but they've got to go find somebody else who can do more and train them properly. I think one of the most important things is to find people who love to come to work and feel part of a winning team. If they get filled up by that, they won't want to leave.

Ted:
Yes, and so when people are growing holistically as a whole being, and they feel like their inherent talents, values, and purpose are being applied fully, they feel in control. With the CDL tools, employees will achieve more financially. By committing to servant leadership, with an entrepreneurial focus on what will grow the company's profitability, there's more to share, and everyone gets some of it. That has to be guaranteed because then people realize they are very happy to commit additional talent and turn their turbochargers on, but they're not going to do it if they feel flatlined at 14 or 15 dollars an hour. No one can even live on that after taxes! This feeling makes people think, *I'll just save my talent for my secondary, personal entrepreneurial activity on the weekends because I need that energy to make myself more money. Not going to give it here.* We have to change that.

CHAPTER 3

CUSTOMER DRIVEN PERFORMANCE ASSESSMENT

Internal and External Customer Feedback is the information guidance system that allows an organization (and human beings) to grow on the intended strategic pathway to achieve its vision. Trying to scale your organization without hearing directly from the customers about how they rate their experience with you is like throwing a dart in the air with your eyes closed and hoping it lands on the bullseye. While you may be well intentioned, you could very well be aiming at the wrong thing, investing time and energy into something your customers care nothing about, and neglecting the real issues which affect your relationship with them. If your customers are the heart of your organization, then you need to ask for their feedback and make adjustments accordingly.

CDL offers a framework which incorporates customer feedback as a crucial piece to optimum growth.

CUSTOMER CAREABOUTS

Customer Careabouts are the critical subset of an internal or external customer's overall set of needs or expectations. We help each client narrow down their customer's set of "Careabouts" to no more than three or four (and you might start with just one). This also takes into account that various clients will have different Careabouts, and having a good understanding of the variety of Careabouts is important to deliver excellence across the board. You don't want to get bogged down in measures of bureaucracy—you want to focus on those needs and expectations which will keep your customers satisfied! This is done by asking the question: *Which aspects of our service or product must achieve a score of 9 or 10 on a 10-point scale in order for you to continue doing business with us?* Generic examples of Customer Careabouts include timeliness, accuracy, effectiveness, and value for money. Here is a hypothetical example: One retailer wants pristine packaging for your computer parts, but another might do the installations for their clients, and so the clients will never see the packaging (hence different Customer Careabouts). In CDL, all Careabouts are turned into objectively measurable actions using numerical scores (e.g. number of deadlines missed this month, or the number of errors in the budget reports to each department, etc.).

Modern business management expert Peter Drucker famously said, "If you can't measure it, you can't improve it." If you measure something, it becomes important. While data collection may not be the sexiest part of CDL, it's an integral piece in articulating values and upholding standards - both for your organization and your customers. If something is important, you need to find a way to measure it because everything boils down to accountability.

The key concept is that we are rated on our ability to deliver on our values, our priorities, and how we serve as an organization. Everyone needs to help drive the organization's mission forward, so everyone is evaluated on the things that matter.

It's easy to get clients on board when the conversation is had ahead of time and it is facilitated in a way where clients see value in the process. It's simply saying, *We want to know that you are being taken care of. I don't want to waste your time, but if you participate, I promise you'll see responsiveness like you've never seen before.* Who *wouldn't* want that?

An example I like to use is of a widget company that has three critical customers. Alpha Constructions Careabout is to never fall below 100 widgets in their warehouse. When they get below 150, we need to ship them out an order of widgets to fill them back up to 250. Bravo Express wants to maintain zero inventory, but if they place an order, they want their client to receive their widgets directly in 24 hours or less. Charlie Custom Parts, unsurprisingly, only orders custom widgets and they need them within seven days. All these clients have unique Customer Careabouts, and if you don't assess their needs and give them each what they value, you won't be fulfilling their uniquely individual needs. When you ask them what is important to you and what complete success looks like to you, you start building a life long relationship focused on their needs… and when their needs change, that potentially gives insight into market trends that others in the industry will take months to notice.

It becomes important to initiate this feedback loop in short cycles because the data will guide where to go next. In a four-week cycle, you can often catch problems at the head, before they escalate. The longer you put the cycle off, the bigger the problems are before they start showing up.

VALUE CHAIN MANAGEMENT

The work processes of all organizations are built around a backbone or spine—the vital chain of action/decision vertebrae through which the central nervous system of operations must flow. This chain must be in a particular order (usually) and each component or link must efficiently and effectively add value to the final output (service or product) at the end of the chain. Aspects of this output are often used as Customer Careabouts by the external customer. This core chain constitutes the series of linked processes from which the organization derives its profit.

In addition to the core Value Chain, there are necessary support services, such as Human Resources, Accounting/Finance, IT, and General Administration. Each of these should provide measurable support to the Value Chain functions.

"So, you've got this upside-down pyramid, with customers at the top, right? The customers are giving us performance reviews, which is a customer benefit of CDL. Let's say, for instance, customers complain that your employees don't pick up the phone fast enough. As soon as we made picking up the phone part of our CDL report card, people were picking up on the first ring. When we made the standard of shipping an item, we were shipping 99.98% accurate every month.

We want everyone to be a part of taking care of our vision on the strategy of the organization. Are you engaged in making the best customer service experience?

Gathering data is the best way to keep everyone on target. It's all about mission success.

Because we do this on a regular basis, we can catch a decline in sales before we have a loss and go negative. When we drop in sales, we come back at a faster trajectory than everyone else, every time one of these things happens. Everyone here knows what to do, and we push for customer experience every day. So, whenever there's a problem, we accelerate and end up in a better position every time."

ANONYMOUS CDL ADVOCATE

EXAMPLE: A SCOTTISH WHISKEY COMPANY

"Lorraine" was a Bottling Hall shift leader responsible for the performance of dozens of women who operate the bottling lines for a leading single malt whiskey and other quality brands produced in Scotland. For decades, women like Lorraine have competently and calmly conducted bottling line operations while facing innumerable frustrations with: line equipment problems, dry goods supply challenges (e.g., the boxes, labels, dividers, bottles), and the availability and quality of liquor provided by the Maturation and Blending Dept. and the Reduction Dept. (in which the strong spirit is mixed with water to achieve the appropriate alcohol percentage).

With CDL in place, they scored the departments in the Value Chain which were responsible for each of their "Careabouts." Namely, Lorraine and the ladies rated the Engineering Department on two Careabouts: 1) bottling line downtime and 2) line changeover time when switching from one brand of product to another on the line. They scored Dry Goods Department on availability and timely delivery of boxes, dividers, labels and bottles to the line. Finally, Lorraine provided scores to the Reduction Department on availability of spirits to the proper line at the proper time. Now, instead of getting excuses or rude remarks from the men in Engineering or Reduction, the incentives have led the men to deliver what the ladies in the line actually "Careabout."

So, what have CDL, Lorraine, and the leaders done for the business bottom line? Amazing things, actually. The departments tracked productivity, efficiency, and wastage. The ladies and their newly supportive gentlemen colleagues reduced bottling line downtime, which saves the organization hundreds of thousands of pounds sterling per year. They increased efficiency and accuracy, thereby reducing the time it takes to run an order and the number of instances of re-work. Finally, they significantly reduced waste of dry goods by working with that department to provide updated, more accurate specifications to vendors on such items as case dividers.

In short, the ladies used their new found CDL Freedom! The Bottling Hall employees learned that they are important managers of the organization Value Chain. They know their place in it and how to get excellent service from the rest of the chain. *Congratulations, ladies!!* Not only that, but due largely to CDL training and procedures, the organization was selected for the "Investors in People Award" by the British government.

CONVERSATIONS WITH TED ANDERS

Daniel:
One of the things I've uncovered in reading your original book is the importance of creating an organization's culture where it's safe to bring concerns forward. It sounds like CDL nurtures just that. CDL doesn't let wounds fester. You deal with issues when they're little cuts.

Ted:
Yes, if a customer has an issue, we need to hear them out and use it as fuel for finding a solution. Likewise, if an employee comes to management with an idea of how things can be done with greater efficiency, we need to listen. Everyone involved should be mature and recognize that we're all here to make a healthy organization, community and nation. The conscious part of that means, *I'm conscious of your needs. I'm conscious of the whole team. I'm conscious of the marketplace and how we're impacting it. I'm conscious of the impact we are having on the planet as we gather our resources in order to do our business. I'm conscious of how we treat suppliers and supply culture.* It comes down to individual relationships, caring for one another, lifting each other up all the way back through the supply chain and all the way forward into the customer marketplace.

Daniel:
Let's say one department of an organization is failing. If you don't have a good system in place of knowing, the problem will escalate. CDL puts a spotlight on the problem areas and then encourages everyone to recognize the problem area and solve it. The culture is not one where people think, *Well, that's not my department. I can't do my job because this department doesn't do theirs.*

Ted:
Exactly! We find out who serves that department, both in terms of management and ownership. We reach out to team colleagues who serve that group in order for them to be able to

meet their promises. We are all on the same page and desire to build more effective leadership, more effective management, more effective resourcing, and more effective building of team skills. If employees don't get that, they can't perform. Pointing fingers, bashing them, and beating them doesn't help anyone. It's also unjustified if teams aren't getting what they need in order to perform. This is why we focus on servant leadership.

Within an entrepreneurial environment, we need to be laser focused on our customers and on profit orientation. There's a timing on non-functionality. If you have resistant people who do not want to participate in self-reflection, in data-driven, self-winding behavior, then there's only so long you can nurture them, especially if they are not responding to coaching and other investments in their success. Usually within about six months, you know who's on board and who is not interested in contributing. After that it's, *I'm sorry. We've done reasonably what can be done. It's all documented, and it's time for you to find your next opportunity so we can find a better-fit team member.*

CHAPTER 4
KEY PERFORMANCE INDICATORS

In the previous chapter, you learned anything that matters to you and your organization must be made measurable. Each person in the Value Chain needs to wholeheartedly represent the organization's values and be held accountable for their role in upholding the vision. You learned how Customer Careabouts are essential to this process. This chapter will explore the simultaneous focus of rewarding those who perform exceptionally well in your organization and those who advance the values and vision of the organization. Typically, these are referred to in business as Key Performance Indicators.

KEY PERFORMANCE INDICATORS

KPIs are the economic "health" indicators tracked by most accounting departments. For example, you might track productivity in terms of output per person or per machine hour. You could track efficiency in terms of the number of employees in relation to gross sales. Other KPIs often used are: ROI-Return on Investment, ROA-Return on Assets, gross profit margin, wastage rates, productivity, etc. KPIs are part of the limitations or "Playing Field" boundaries placed on CDL Freedom.

> Incentives turn everybody into an entrepreneur, and that is what we tell people—you're getting the profits. At the end of the year, we take 20% of our profits, and we give it to everyone inside the organization. True, it's not done equally. It's done on an equation where $1 salary is worth a point in the bucket. Then there's multipliers based on what level of influence you have (contributions). At the end of the day, everyone receives really good checks.
>
> By using CDL, employees are evaluated and based on their service (i.e., their Careabouts scores) and their impact on economic KPIs. KPIs can and should be tied to one or more "Customer Careabouts" so everyone can see that by focusing on the internal and external Customer Careabouts, the KPIs improve.
>
> They get a measurement every six weeks (we started at four weeks as recommended, but after using CDL for

25 years, this is what is working for us now), but their check is paid every quarter. Therefore, they are getting nice little pieces during the year. It's spread out, so if we ever have a slowdown and we're not making a lot of profit, it's all balanced. You are still getting income from the previous months. Using this system, we've never had a negative month.

ANONYMOUS CDL ADVOCATE

THE RELATIONSHIP BETWEEN "CAREABOUTS" AND KPIs

We believe it is critical—and possible—to correlate almost all primary Customer Careabouts with one or more economic KPIs. Surprising though it may be, there are still boards of directors and chief financial officers who aren't sure which comes first: external and internal customer satisfaction or financial results (KPIs). We wholeheartedly believe that in order to achieve sustained high scores on critical internal and external Customer Careabouts, people who work in a CDL servant leadership environment make processes operate in the most efficient, effective, and reliable way. The financial by-products of their voluntary improvement efforts are the stronger economic KPIs.

The old-fashioned management model of butt-kicking for efficiencies and higher profit margin just won't work on a long-term basis. Certainly, such an approach never leads to discretionary, innovative stretching on the part of employees.

Any improvements made by staff in the old butt-kicking model tend to be short-lived, fraught with damage to personnel, and ultimately very expensive as the organization spends money on "triage" solutions.

Is it really possible to make profit and do good for others at the same time? Let's take a look at the following real-life example and you can decide for yourself.

EXAMPLE: HOME HEALTH CARE COMPANY

Janet, Betty, and Susan (names have been changed) were nursing supervisors at a home health care organization. They were tasked with two objectives: 1) provide excellent home health care according to Medicare guidelines and 2) increase organization profits. While these objectives sound straightforward, there were several obstacles in their path to success.

First of all, Janet, Betty, and Susan, and the rest of their nursing colleagues had never been trained, nor required to think about the profit-making side of patient-care delivery. In fact, because they went into nursing for the human service and caring aspects, they even resented administrators and managers who tried to get them to focus on the business side of patient care. In addition to this typical, traditional impasse, which exists in most health care organizations, Janet, Susan, and Betty faced another obstacle. Under Medicare guidelines, it is illegal to promote or "sell" services to physicians. You can't market your home health business just to increase your patient visit rate. The physician must independently decide to refer his or her existing cases to the home health provider, as it is illegal to try to push up the home visit count just to increase billings. So, the supervisors were faced with a serious dilemma. They knew it was necessary to help the corporation make more money in order to have the best facilities, staff, and services and still yield a respectable profit to shareholders. Yet, Medicare regulations, and their own staff attitudes, prohibited them from promoting an increase in visits, which was the main source of revenue. How did we coach them through this dilemma?

Ted worked with his colleague Beverly Fisher, and they oriented the supervisors and staff to the CDL Freedom Formula and analyzed their work. The organization agreed they had two customer groups: 1) the patients and their families and 2) the referring physicians. For the first "customer" group, Susan, Betty, Janet, and the field nurses knew quite well what the "Careabouts" were. From their years of experience, they could tell you immediately that patients and their families wanted thorough, timely, professional and caring, in-home nursing services at the appropriate level of care. The piece of the puzzle they weren't so sure of was the set of physicians' Careabouts.

They knew that their efforts to build cooperative relationships by bringing cookies and coffee mugs to the doctors' offices was not improving work relationships and communications between nurses and physicians. Clearly, they needed a new perspective on their physicians as customers. We helped them get a fresh perspective by training them to apply creative, "right-brained" strategies to the problem—as well as giving them a solid overview of the basic principles of business profit and loss. They applied these new skills to determine the physicians' most important Careabouts, while also relating them to corporate revenue growth (a KPI) within the Medicare constraints.

The solution turned out to be quite simple. The physicians all had busy practices and didn't really see the home healthcare patients very often. Also, the nurses were overloaded with paperwork about patients. So, it was a routine embarrassment for most physicians to hear from a patient's family member inquiring about mother's or grandmother's health. They were often embarrassed because they really weren't up to date on Granny's exact treatment or condition. They really cared about having simple, quick reference information on all their home health patients so they would always be well informed in front of Granny's family.

To serve physicians on this Careabout, we created bright, neon-yellow patient status sheets with a quick update on Granny's condition. The sheets were produced as a result of a redesigned patient care planning process we called "The Care Team Conferencing Process". A standardized process produced a patient summary sheet which was given to the physician each week. He or she could quickly find it among the papers on their desk when a family member called. Not only did the family feel more informed, the doctors began to see the need for more comprehensive treatment approvals for the patients. These treatment increases were legitimate services to which the patients were entitled under Medicare guidelines. As a result of more timely updates on Granny's condition, the patient received more comprehensive care and the home health care organization made more money. The physicians were so satisfied with the improved communications from the nurses that they began to refer more patients to the organization. The organization experienced legitimate, dramatic revenue growth (4.8 million dollars in increased revenue after just six months over an 18-month flatline) and patients received more comprehensive care. That is a win-win-win situation, if there ever was one!

MONTHLY ASSESSMENTS

Part of the reason CDL is so successful is because of its standardized habits. Consistent, regular assessments, and regular, creative, process improvements are crucial to CDL's proactive power. No one wants to hear about a problem that has gotten large and looming. We want to spot potential issues before they arise and get ahead of the game. This is why maintaining a monthly assessment cycle is a key component of the process.

In Ted's capacity as an organizational psychologist, he noted that regular, specific assessments are something most organizations do poorly. Even if your leader is great, if the structure of evaluating employees is terrible or inconsistent, the growth of your organization will be stagnant. As stated, the Key Performance Indicators you choose to assess should be based upon your organization's core values and on customer feedback. Decision making, communication, professionalism, and performance are often high on the list. The beauty of CDL is that the process sets clear expectations, empowers teams to manage themselves, and makes leaders accountable to helping them deliver for their customers.

Ted teaches what he calls the *3-Step Monthly CDL Habit*, which encourages organizations to carve out time to analyze data and performance.

1. Collect numerical scores (feedback) from customers (internal and external)

2. Conduct 45-minute standard CDL score and process-review meetings with every team—and then bring the whole company together for a summary of key learnings and new action items:

    a. Energize
    b. Acknowledge high scores
    c. Plan improvement of low scores
    d. Assign actions

3. Apply competitive, Customer-Driven process and relationship improvement actions throughout the next month

Using the following charts as an example, you can begin to imagine what the monthly data collection for your organization might look like. The first chart (Diagram 3, on the following pages) is the simplest version, as it has only Customer Careabouts on it. The second chart (Diagram 4, on the following pages) is a bit more complex and powerful for the organization because the chart also includes the economic KPIs. Remember, measurement of Careabouts and KPIs (which have been thoughtfully correlated in the CDL planning process) are essential. Indeed, the more you can show causality between high scores and Careabouts and resultant KPIs, the more powerful your results will be for the organization's growth and health.

CUSTOMER DRIVEN LEADERSHIP

Customer Driven Performance Team Assessment Chart
A Customer Driven Leadership™ Tool
(To track how well an organizational department/team serves external clients or internal departments/teams)

Name of Service Provider: _____ Name of Team being Evaluated _____ Month/Year: Dec 2022 Tracked by: Name of Team's Scorekeeping

Customer	Careabout	Description	How Measured	How Collected	Work Process (KPI)	Last Score	Weight	0	2.5	5	7.5	10	Average Score
Paying customers & other departments	1. Better Communication	Emails with project status updates	2 x week, on Wed. or Fri. by 4p.m. (# per month)	Department scorekeeping retains email log	Project status reporting process	3	2		<4	4	5-6 6	7-8	9+	5 x 2 = 10
Paying customers & other departments	2. Projects completed on-time	Projects that missed deadlines by days late for all projects tracked by month	Sum of all days late for all projects tracked by month	Department leadership maintains log	Project timeliness reporting process	6	3		>3	3 3	2	1	0	2.5 x 3 = 7.5
Who you serve with this Careabout	#. Careabout name	What really matters?	How will we measure success?	How will we know how successful we are?	What process is being improved? Linked to KPIs	Last score	How important is this?			The actual break down scores...				points x weighting = score

There may be many more Careabouts being tracked for a single team, owed to a variety of different teams/customers...
We recommend that you start with 1 (for each key organization or customer the team serves) and grow as you mature in the process

Explanatory Notes (Use this space to explain any item or procedure above)   Follow CDL SOP to turn in Charts   Overall Score*: 3.5

Overall Score Calculation (10+7.5)=17.5/5(Careabout weightings)= 3.5

* Multiply each category's points by the weighting and sum the totals, then divide by the sum of Careabout weightings to find Overall Score

Diagram 3

SNAP THIS CODE TO SEE THIS AND OTHER FORMS
AT CUSTOMERDRIVENLEADERSHIP.CO/RESOURCES

Key Performance Indicators

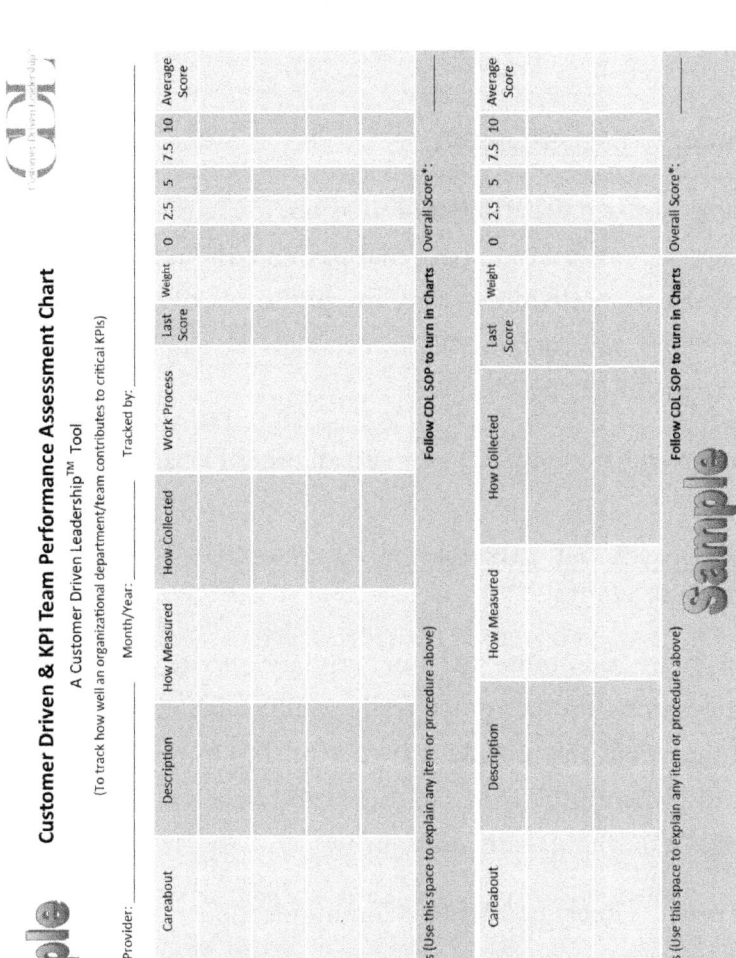

Diagram 4

CDL CONCEPTS FROM DIAGRAMS 3 & 4

Category 1: CUSTOMER

In the case of a department or division, the "customer" can be either the organization's external paying customer or another department or division—or both. In the case of an individual supervisor or leader, the "customers" are the employees in the department or division.

Example: External Customer and all other Departments

Category 2: THE CUSTOMER "CAREABOUTS" (critical needs or wants)

These are the three or four primary service or product expectations the customer really, really cares about, out of all the things the provider may do for the customer. In other words, when "push comes to shove" and time is of the essence, these "Careabouts" are top priority.

Example: Timely or "Better" Communication

Category 3: OPERATIONAL DEFINITION

This describes WHAT the Careabout is exactly.

Example: Customers receive email updates on active projects.

Category 4: CURRENT PERFORMANCE BASELINE

HOW it will be measured... in specific, observable behavioral terms.

Example: Twice a week, on Wednesday and Fridays, not later than 4:00 p.m. (# of updates per month).

Category 5: MONTHLY DATA COLLECTION PROCEDURE

How, specifically, will our department collect feedback from or on behalf of the customer at the end of the month? This procedure must be the simplest possible activity or it won't get done in most organizations. Plan a technique that has minimal impact on the customer's time and on staff time. Keep it simple but insightful and valid.

Example: The department secretary reviews the email log for each customer and averages the department's performance across all customers for the month. She places this score on a large copy of the Customer Driven Performance Assessment Chart located in a conspicuous place in the department work area. We refer to these posting areas as CDL Performance Tracking Stations.

Category 6: WORK RELATED PROCESS

This is simply a label for the series of tasks that make up the work done to achieve a high score on the Customer

Careabout. This is the process, which would be studied for improvement if the scores are low. You can also list which KPIs tie to this process.

Example: "Status Reporting" Process - KPI Satisfaction

Category 7: CURRENT PERFORMANCE BASELINE

How well have you been meeting this Careabout? The answer provides a starting point for setting monthly scoring credits. Generally, you put current or average historical performance at a credit of 2.5 and then see if you can get better than that in the months ahead. Of course, if processes are not under control, scores may actually fall below 2.5.

Example: The past six months' average is approximately three emails per month (which in the sample would provide 0 points).

Category 8: WEIGHT

This is a determination of how important this Careabout is in relation to the other three to four that the department is tracking on behalf of its customers. One way to determine the relative weighting of a particular Careabout is to determine its demands on department resources or the potential impact on client retention if not done well.

Category 9: SCOREBOARD

This is the measure of customer satisfaction, which will be used to determine department incentive recognitions. Essentially, this breaks down how many points you get for specific levels of services.

Category 10: AVERAGE SCORE

Your Average Score on an individual Customer Careabout is equal to Weight X Points. Your Overall Score is equal to the sum of the Careabout Average Scores / the sum of the Careabout weightings.

Example: For Diagram 3 Careabout 1 the Weight was 2 and the Points was 5 (because we had 6 email updates during the month on our project status) for a total of 10. Our Overall Score 3.5; (10+7.5 the sum of Average Scores) = 17.5/5(sum of Careabout weightings 2+3) = 3.5

The preceding examples of Customer Driven Performance Assessment charts show the most basic forms. After just a few months of practice, the content can become much more challenging. As you advance, one critical addition to the charts is a section which tracks and measures the organization economic Key Performance Indicators. Remember, it is not enough for employees to take care of the paying customer—they must also take care of the owner/shareholder "customers". With this responsibility in mind, most CDL practitioners use the advanced form included here as Diagram 4.

The primary addition to the basic form is the lower section of the chart, which tracks two or three basic financial measures. In this case it is unnecessary to list the KPI as part of the Work Process field of the top part of the chart. For example, a KPI measure could be "staffing", and then you would list which Careabouts deal with staffing and the key metrics involved.

Measures often included are:

- Sales per employee
- Cost of goods sold
- Other costs of doing business
- Gross margin before taxes

The terms determine which "Customer Careabout" on the upper portion of the chart will likely correlate with a constructive, significant impact on one or more of the KPIs. Then, a simple correlation can be calculated between the improvement in Customer Careabout score (e.g., lower errors on the production line) and for example, a decrease in the costs of doing business.

While such correlations may seem elementary to a sophisticated leader, we find that most employees are not in the habit of concerning themselves with such "business ownership" issues on a regular basis. One thing is sure, the more often employees think like owners, the more likely it is the business will be well run—by "self-winding", incentivized teams with which any shareholders and customers would be satisfied.

CONVERSATIONS WITH TED ANDERS

Daniel:

When it comes to performance, all of us are ultimately responsible for each other. Whether you're the person at the bottom or top of the Value Chain, we are responsible for everything. Is this accurate?

Ted:

Yes. One of the things that happens when folks begin to take responsibility is they look at themselves and realize, *I'm not currently capable of achieving this commitment or this promise that my role/department has made to corporate success.* First of all, you need to own that reality and secondly, decide if the required capability or action potential can be developed in you and your team, but if you can't, because of timing or because of priorities with other work, then you employ the power of encouraging and measuring a "volunteerism" culture where there may be some folks in the organization who can pick up that piece of work. Maybe it doesn't even require that person leaving their other position. The team just says, *I'll come help you for a few hours a week.* The person who has a weakness but has a strength elsewhere can also go volunteer to help somebody else. We want to see that kind of non-threatening sharing of talent. That's very important.

Daniel:
I've done that in my own career. I got so good at a job that it was routine for me, but then I got an opportunity to see how I could help another team and started volunteering my time there. I volunteered more and more of my time, and eventually I ended up transferring to that team, but that was primarily on my initiative. In a CDL environment, you're aware of the gifts and talents of the whole organization, and you can plug and play at some level. It becomes about finding opportunities where people can be drawn to areas where they're gifted. Right?

Ted:
Right. But people can't just talk about it. This assessment needs to become a monthly habit, where the entire organization comes together for a few hours and reviews the Customer Driven Leadership Performance Assessment Charts. You need to make a habit of asking, "Where are there process problems?" "Who can help that team or that person improve?" "We're not going to attack the person." "We're going to say, *the process currently is not optimal.*" The solution may require some volunteerism. It may require a temporary reassignment of a couple of folks to that team to help get the process improved. When the score is up, employees may end up going back to their original teams or we may discover, *Wow, we didn't even know that person had those skills! We don't have to go out and hire someone. We can simply make an internal change.* Now everyone is happier and people are growing all the time. We're

not going to fire or get rid of anyone, so long as they are taking consistent baby steps forward in their performance.

Daniel:
Have you seen an organization expending resources on Quality Assurance (QA) that have been able to let go of that or moving to repurpose those people? If everyone in the organization is fully invested in making sure the quality is where it needs to be, do you just eliminate those positions?

Ted:
You rarely need to get rid of employees. You just make them more useful to the bottom line of the organization. So many organizations, especially entrepreneurial-owned organizations, really resent overhead people like Human Resources (HR) and QA. It's debatable how much value they're adding in terms of the bottom line and final net profit. When they're powerful, trained well, accurate and constructive, then they really are worth their money. But in a lot of places, it's simply lip service being done. Are they really pervasive in the hearts and minds and daily behavior of everyone? Usually not.

And so, yes, when you go into an organization to do CDL, where there is an existing HR department or QA department, and the organization is not, in fact, doing its best, (achieving an amazing reputation in the marketplace or thriving financially) then clearly, those departments could be given some new tools to make a difference. We try to help them understand they are no longer just hiring, doing paychecks, and looking at some sort of quality data coming back from observations of processes. They are actually going to start running a monthly data-driven, constant improvement, customer-driven culture in which they will become largely responsible for coaching and maintaining a new culture—the culture of pervasive entrepreneurship and customer, data-driven decision making. If you're going to start driving the economic KPIs of an organization, all of a sudden, HR and QA become essential to driving the overall value of the organization. They are no longer just a compliance "overhead" cost. Shareholders love this additional value for the funds expended on these functions.

Daniel:
So really, every single person in the organization has a job that is clearly defined and valued, and everyone makes sure the customer is going to be satisfied at the end?

Ted:
Yes, and that means QA and HR have coordinated together to make sure the right people, the right staff development with the CDL tools, the right economic consequences in the CDL model are, in fact, in place and are happening in a timely monthly habit pattern.

As a result, HR begins to find greater talent from inside the organization, which is much less expensive than trying to bring someone in from outside. When they begin to see from the Customer Driven Leadership Monthly Score Charts, they notice which specific behaviors actually produce a satisfied colleague or a satisfied customer. Well, then you start hiring based on that chart, and it's a different hiring process. It's not just *Oh, do you have a degree in x? And have you worked in this field before?* It's, *Can you prove to us you can help add value to these five processes, which are the core of that department's success? If you can't, we can't hire you.*

Furthermore, the teams themselves actually begin doing the jobs for HR. HR can select new staff to be considered through the various ways of finding talent to employ, but after they've done a basic background check and some basic review of the person, they should turn that person over to the team for another interview and final decision. It shouldn't be HR hiring for a successful green level team. The green level team should hire their own people because they know exactly how to ask them. Teams don't want to hire anybody that can't help them get 10s on a scale of zero to ten. If they do, their scores are going to drop and their monthly take home is going to go down.

Essentially, HR should become the center of holistic staff development, holistic process improvement, holistic quality applications, so that everyone knows how to be their best. Now HR/QA have become the coaches of people and processes that don't have 10s yet. The new goal is to provide them with the support, the resources, and the skills they need to make 10s. Everything becomes laser focused and, all of a sudden, HR/QA are no longer overhead. They are actually the drivers of behaviors that cause the organization to grow.

Daniel:
And that might mean HR becomes more of a coach towards talent growth. I think that's very positive. Coaching is a great tool to develop talent at every level of an organization. Ideally, HR should get to know the teams—where their strengths and weaknesses are, how to help them with their weaknesses, how to get the most out of their strengths or bring in outside coaches and consultants to do that work.

Ted:
Participating in their monthly CDL score and process review meetings and seeing a process which keeps delivering a RED score for three months is not good enough. That's when the leadership needs to say, *I'm not here to criticize. I'm here to help you. Let's see where your processes don't work well, and let's see what resources, skills, talents, etc. we need in order to get up to a GREEN score.* That's when people know they're not coming to criticize; they're coming in to help. And when the team moves from RED to YELLOW, everyone celebrates with them. It becomes such a positive way of going to work, being together, and trending upwards together.

CHAPTER 5

THE GEOMETRICS OF CUSTOMER DRIVEN LEADERSHIP

As an employee, how many times did you have a fantastic idea which could have significantly strengthened the organization, and the leadership team wouldn't listen? Those employees who are on the ground are often the ones who have the most relevant, innovative ideas because they are the first to spot potential problems. An organization's ceiling for success is often contingent on how much autonomy they give employees within an accountability framework.

Let's say your organization sells widgets and the client typically wants 100 widgets in his warehouse at all times, but all of a sudden, his request drops down to 50. Because of the Customer Careabouts, you've already established an open dialogue with the client. You are comfortable reaching out and saying, "We want to make sure we're delivering exactly what you need. What's changed?" The client discloses that a competitor has moved right next door and has taken half his clients.

A proactive employee will immediately understand the conversation that needs to happen at this moment, so they can assist the client in getting ahead of market trends. *What service do you need? What are you looking for? What's attracting people to the competitor's business?* A self-winding team not only can initiate this dialogue but can custom create a service which may not only serve this particular client but other clients as well.

If you're really assessing what your clients need on a continual basis, you are less likely to be blindsided or have someone acting faster than you in taking care of them.

Because CDL has created a culture of accountability and innovation, this same employee can now go to her leadership with not only a concern but a potential solution.

With each application of Customer Driven Leadership, we have learned how to help organizations get ever more powerful thorough results. The result of our "lessons learned" is to connect the Customer Driven Leadership Freedom Formula with two other essential business improvement activities: The "Playing Field" of limits such as targeted KPIs, along with an investment in "Personal and Team Power." Let me use an analogy to elaborate just a bit.

If we think of CDL Freedom Formula as the entrepreneurial motor, then the organization or organizational structure is the car. This car has certain constraints within which it can perform. It has to have a relatively smooth surface on which to operate. It needs a certain amount and type of fuel. It can only accommodate so many passengers and their baggage. You get the point. You cannot be all things to all people. You have to make tradeoffs, such as, which is more important? Speed or luggage capacity? Luxury or affordable?

Well, an organization has the same type of constraints. Ted Anders calls these the "Playing Field" limits in which the CDL Freedom Formula must operate. In addition to the motor (CDL Freedom Formula) and the car (the "Playing Field of organizational constraints"), a high-performance fuel and lubrication is needed. Therefore, an investment in personal and team power is essential. An individual's personal power and capability serves as the high-octane fuel and performance lubricant needed to run a fast-paced, hot, competitive race. When blended with the CDL Freedom Formula (the inverted triangle), we refer to this unique, powerful combination as The Geometrics of CUSTOMER DRIVEN LEADERSHIP approach to creating sustainable organizational success. See Diagram 5.

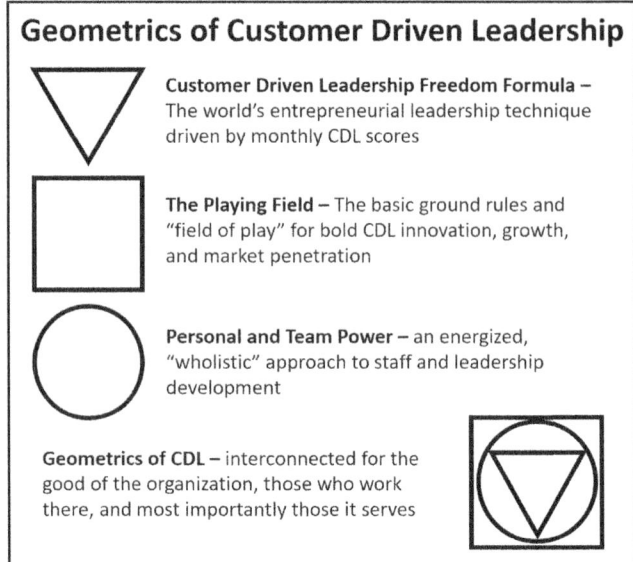

Diagram 5

The major focus of this discussion is the "Playing Field" (Constraints and KPIs). When you get this part right, a mature balance between Customer Careabouts and the organization's needs can be obtained. Employees and leaders can get maximum power and results from Customer Driven Leadership Freedom Formula when the organization's "playing field" is well defined for all players. The reason this is true is quite simple. When we know our operating boundaries, our decision-making is usually more confident. Therefore, we have more confidence in making innovative improvement suggestions. When we know where the chalk lines are on the Playing Field, we can play boldly right up to the line—but not cross it. When the boundaries are not clear, it's like walking along the edge of a cliff in a dense fog. We stay as far away from the edge as we can. When we're that unsure of our footing, how many employees or leaders are going to champion bold, fast-paced, entrepreneurial improvements? They're going to be more likely to stay in the center of the Playing Field rather than "on the edge." Such mediocre posturing makes for a losing team. Many professional sports teams end up losing a big game with a "playing it safe" strategy even when they have a huge lead. A better strategy is to continually strengthen your lead and adapt to the environment.

We have found that some of the most critical Playing Field boundaries are:

- Organizational Plans – e.g. your Strategic, Business, Marketing, Sales and Advertising Plans (i.e. The Big Picture and the Promise to Customers)
- Legalities, Ethics, Values
- Process and Equipment Constraints
- Cost/Expense and target Profit Margin

The key for leaders is to judge when to widen the Playing Field and loosen the limits. This situation is not unlike how our parents needed to treat us when we were kids. I remember when I was four. It was OK to play in my own yard but not go down the street to a neighbor's yard by myself. However, at age five, when I had demonstrated good decision-making and obedience to the rules, I was allowed to go over to a neighbor's yard to play, and it felt great! The Playing Field boundary had been stretched to allow for our expanded need to explore and create. By the time I reached age seven or eight, I was allowed to ride my bike around the neighborhood or go to a neighbor's house a couple of blocks away. The world had really opened up for me. What a Playing Field! Maybe you can relate to expanding boundaries from where and when you grew up, and as we grew, the boundaries and responsibilities just kept on getting bigger the more experience we acquired. That's the step-by-step approach that most work forces need to experience, as they are asked to widen the field of responsibility for greater growth and improvement required to succeed in the modern and quickly changing world.

Each area of play has a specific objective and each employee knows exactly what their team's objectives are. *This is what I'm responsible for and what I'm supposed to accomplish.* Having that specific definition is powerful because employees know exactly what they are being evaluated on and can make a checklist to ensure their own success. When teams are told expectations upfront and are not meeting those goals, they are quick to spot an issue and explore possible solutions.

An example of a Playing Field outline comes from one of our clients in the United Kingdom, an engineering firm. We will call them Echo Engineering. The staff did a fine job of clarifying the limits within which they could conduct organizational improvement. Their diagram, as well as a flowchart of how to challenge one of their limits, is included below.

Example #1

The Echo Engineering example (Diagram 6, below) shows major boundary categories and "bulleted" sub-boundaries, which have to be taken into account before making changes to processes, structures, budgets, staffing, etc. For example, employees in the manufacturing division could decide that changes needed to be made in the resources category. Perhaps machine tools were outdated or inadequate to produce consistent quality standards required to become an approved vendor to a certain customer. However, the staff knows they cannot make significant changes to the machine tools until they have determined the impact on other Playing Field constraints. Specifically, it is likely that their leaders will ask them to first take into account other factors such as the impact of any financial expenditures on the margins. The staff must be able to show that the capital expenditure for new machine tools will lead to less waste and increased sales to certain clients so that the investment can be recovered within an acceptable financial time frame. The staff might also need to determine if an equipment change would have an impact on Health and Safety Law or Quality Procedures. In addition, people might need training before becoming proficient with the new equipment. This would be an additional impact on the Resources category.

This is the sophisticated thinking that CDL teams learn to do within a matter of months. They begin to really act like owners of the business—especially when their own decisions can directly impact their monthly CDL scores and their incentives.

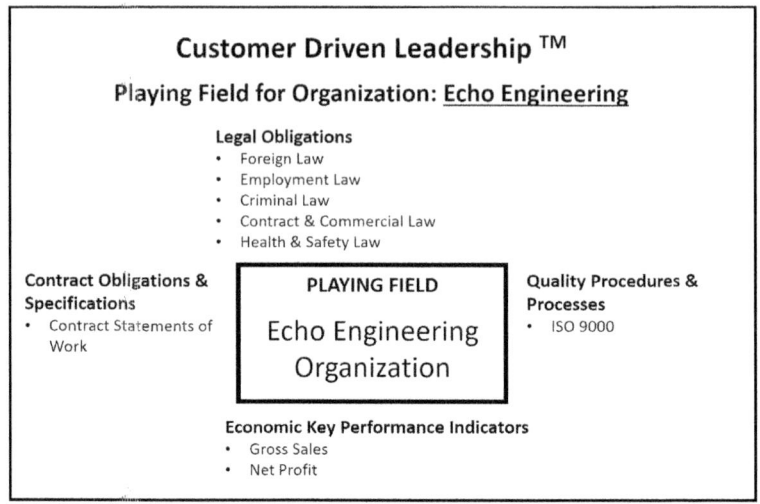

Diagram 6

EXAMPLE #2

The second example of a Playing Field includes generic, critical boundaries (Diagram 7). We sometimes ask our clients to use these boundaries just to be sure essential planning and thinking has been done—or gets done soon! As you can see, we have our clients clarify their organization's Strategic Plan to everyone and point out how each department can measurably contribute to the achievement of the plan. Secondly, we coach them to clarify their Business Plan—including departmental budgets and other financial KPIs. Third, we suggest they clarify the Marketing Plan and ensure that everyone understands how it is integrated with the Strategic and Business Plans.

With these three plans in place, the macro and micro-business processes that are essential to success can be identified. These four areas then constitute the Playing Field on which everyone can design their personal and team "plays" to achieve high internal or external customer scores on a monthly basis.

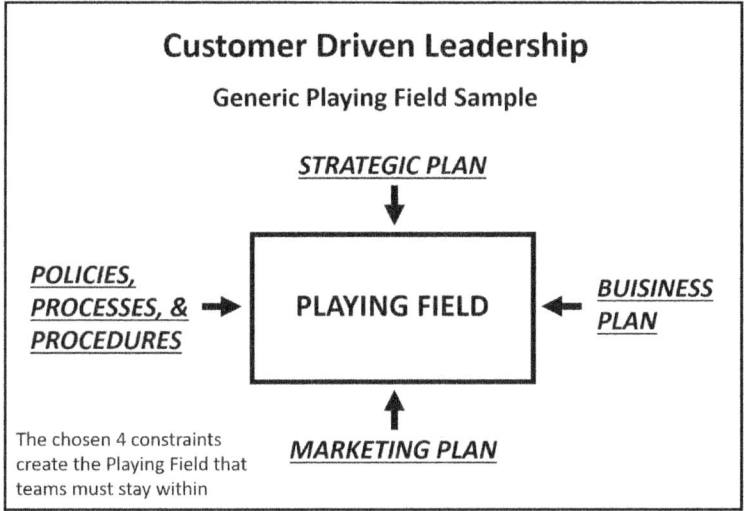

Diagram 7

We could include several more examples, but it would probably be a good idea at this time to practice an example for yourself. Below is an example of a blank Playing Field for you to explore (Diagram 8).

Remember, the constraints are the boundaries which cannot be crossed and still achieve a healthy financial contribution to the organization.

```
┌─────────────────────────────────────────────────────────┐
│           Customer Driven Leadership ™                  │
│  Organization: _____        │
│                                                         │
│              Constraint #1: _____             │
│              _____             │
│              _____             │
│                                                         │
│                  ┌──────────────────┐                   │
│  Constraint #2:  │  PLAYING FIELD   │  Constraint #4:   │
│  _____   │                  │  _____  │
│  _____   │ Team or Department: │ _____  │
│  _____   │                  │  _____  │
│                  └──────────────────┘                   │
│                                                         │
│              Constraint #3: _____             │
│              _____             │
│              _____             │
│                                                         │
│  Fill in the 4 constraints to create the Playing Field  │
└─────────────────────────────────────────────────────────┘
```

Diagram 8

Here's how these Playing Fields are applied in a CDL environment. Remember the third element of the CDL Freedom Formula? It involves a monthly team problem-solving session focused on improving the lowest customer scores. Teams should be taught to use process-improvement tools and other decision-making skills. These sessions are referred to as monthly "CDL Score Review and Process Improvement Sessions."

Here is an abbreviated example of some of the discussion which should take place in one of these meetings:

The leader might lead a discussion saying, "OK, folks. We've just brainstormed a list of possible improvements, which could lead to a higher score from our customer. Before we vote on a particular course of action to improve our customer scores next month, let's ask ourselves one or more of the following questions based on our Playing Field reminders.

1. Is the change or improvement action clearly 'in sync' with the company's Strategic Plan? Which element of the plan does it support?
2. Does our proposed action meet budget guidelines, growth targets, efficiency targets or other KPIs?

More specifically, can we answer 'Yes' to at least one of the following questions about our proposed action? These questions help us determine if the action we choose will help build asset value for the organization.

Asset Value Contribution Questions (suggested by Des Benjamin, a CDL expert based in Australia) look specifically at the monetary considerations of an action.

- Does the action increase sales?
- Does the action increase margin?
- Does the action reduce the cost of operation (i.e. increase efficiency)?

If we can't answer 'Yes' to at least one of these questions, then we probably shouldn't consider the action based on its ability to improve the bottom line.

As the preceding team discussion scenario shows, your Playing Field boundaries prompt department teams to take into account a variety of "business ownership" factors. When they think like business owners, there is a reduced risk of their improvement attempts backfiring and having a negative impact on the organization. Over time, as teams build a track record of making independent, innovative—sometimes bold—changes while staying within safety boundaries, leaders become more confident about letting go of authority and resource control. The increasing maturity of the teams creates freedom for leaders to get their noses out of the mire of micro-management and back onto visioning, market penetration, and global competitiveness. Isn't that change worth a lot to an organization? Ultimately, it could mean the difference between stagnation and growth, survival or death.

This steady broadening of the Playing Field for staff helps the organization move from a stagnant, unhealthy RED environment, through cautious change and improvement actions in what we call the YELLOW, to a bold, "go-getting" Entrepreneurial GREEN machine. (Note: The colors of traffic lights are internationally recognized so we use them to communicate CDL readiness status: STOP, CAUTION, OR GO). This GREEN maturation of the corporate culture is what companies around the world have been trying to achieve. The Playing Field helps support and stabilize the maturation process into a full-fledged CDL entrepreneurial environment.

ACCOUNTABILITY TO THE TEAM

Data and feedback are collected externally through Customer Careabouts, as we know. It's equally important to ensure accountability of service and promote servant leadership through internal data collection. Some clients call this process "Community Careabouts". Everybody through the Value Chain has a regular opportunity to anonymously evaluate their peers and their leaders, providing tangible, constructive feedback. This values employees by asking them how their teammates are supporting our vision and our organization's values. It also gives leadership insight into who are contributing best within an organization and who are not supporting the team and its empowerment. Bottom line is it asks people to evaluate you on, *Are you someone who is uplifting the team or dragging it down?*

As we were building out the part of the Customer Driven Leadership application for scoring for Community Careabouts, I recommended to Ted that before the scoring period was open that there was an opportunity to add in some bullets of self-reflection for how you feel you best supported the team during the period (a suggestion that he liked).

This gives employees an opportunity to call out their unique contributions. For example, this month I supported the team by:

- Caught a major mistake before we shipped to one of our major clients
- Provided insight to another employee on a phishing email preventing them from clicking
- Worked a double to cover Mikey when his wife was sick and they couldn't find a babysitter

This helps my teammates consider where I think I am adding value before they score me, maybe they would have been unaware of most or some of these things I think are important, or maybe they will think that what I listed was insignificant and did not really tie very much to the team's overall success. Whichever way it is scored there will be a record of what I said I did and how much my teammates thought I contributed.

> "We love Community Careabouts because it's a direct measure of how well we take care of each other and how well we are taking care of the organization's vision. We want everyone to be actively involved in carrying out the vision and strategy, so we ask for feedback. Are you engaged in making our customer service top notch? Would your peers agree with you? When people know their peers will be asked to evaluate, that's the best way to keep everyone on target.
>
> In using this system, we are rewarding virtuous behavior in the workplace. People begin to think, *Oh, you're going to pay me for being nice. I can do that.*
>
> We all have a bad day once in a while but if you have a bad week or a bad month, you know you're going to get written up for that.
>
> In the Community Careabout, we ask peer review questions such as:
> - Does this person help me do my job?
> - Will this person take credit for another's work?
>
> Each team's questions have evolved to suit their needs. HR has access to the Community Careabouts

and will have the necessary follow up conversations. All feedback is anonymous, so no one is penalized for their honesty. And guess what? You get a change in behavior."

ANONYMOUS CDL ADVOCATE

In addition to upholding the organization's core values, employees also know that Community Careabouts are a sure-fire way to get promoted from within and move up the Value Chain.

In order for employees to buy into this method of accountability, the opportunity for feedback must reach all levels of the Value Chain, which means even the top leaders are subjected to the process. How well do ideas move up the chain? How often do they get stuck? Do you feel valued?

CROSS-TEAM SCORES

In addition to individual evaluation, it can be helpful to implement a team score and incentivize with KPIs based on team performance. What this means, as we pull it all together, is in the Value Chain of Team A -> Team B -> Team C we will have the following scores for Team B:

- How well Team B delivered Careabouts for Team C (scored on Team B's success)

- How well Team A delivered Careabouts for Team B (scored on Team A's success, which is important because Team B may have failed to deliver to Team C because it did not get the support it needed from Team A, such as having enough product available)
- How well each member of Team B was scored by peers on community Careabouts (this could be a full team or sampling anonymized score; this helps us to see who is best contributing to the success within the team)
- How well Teams A and C score Team B in being a good partner in delivering success for the organization

The next page shows an example of an Employee Driven Performance Leadership Assessment Chart (Diagram 9) which tracks how well leaders serve their teams.

SNAP THIS CODE TO SEE THIS AND OTHER FORMS
AT CUSTOMERDRIVENLEADERSHIP.CO/RESOURCES

The Geometrics of Customer Driven Leadership

Diagram 9

"CDL, beyond a shadow of a doubt, has a huge return on investment. Because it's a great operating system, it requires some work to get it going and to find the right questions you want on your individual team member report card and also for your team report cards.

It's effective to have two report cards because in the way our organization has structured performance reviews, the team report card counts as up to 8% of your salary for an average score of 10 "across the board" on your individual CDL chart. For the team report card, everybody on the team gets the same grade. For instance, the logistics team gets the same grade on shipping accuracy based on certain things that have to get done each day. Why? Because we want the whole team to share in their success and failures. But then we also recognize individualism.

When a team shares a score, they are the ones invested to solve the problems together. Everybody has pride of ownership in doing the right thing.

One of the problems we experienced in the past was when a team captain didn't take ownership of the entire process. Sometimes leaders would only take ownership of the prize, not the ugly side of the things which require improvement. In CDL culture, you are never shamed for an ugly result. You'll only get praised for revealing a problem and using creative and analytical thought to remove the problem in as sensible and expedient manner as possible. The opposite is also true. If you want to take credit for some gold that wasn't yours, it is not going to stay secret, and it will come at a heavy cost to you. That's just a bad place to be in spiritually, but it's also destructive for a business.

All teams are important because we are a chain. If the chain has a weak link, we all fail together."

ANONYMOUS CDL ADVOCATE

This is one of the most brilliant aspects of CDL. I have witnessed very successful teams where someone was not pulling their weight. For the team to finish the race on three tires, it has to do some emergency and high-risk driving. Maybe they still "win the race." For example, they got a good team score, but how many months can people cover for someone who is not contributing. The Community Careabouts will highlight where the problem is, and the person that is struggling or disengaged (perhaps legitimately) can get the mentoring, coaching, or counseling they need to become successful, or they can be moved to a better-suited position (maybe at another organization or maybe just elsewhere in ours). Resentment does not build; the team pulls together in the short-term when they need to, but individuals not being a good fit or who are having life struggles are also documented monthly and positive action can be taken, and the team will grow healthier month after month, and most importantly, driving on THREE tires does not become "Business as Usual" on the team.

CONVERSATIONS WITH TED ANDERS

Daniel:

Can you give us a couple of examples of what a self-winding team looks like? Can you provide some best-use cases where the implementation of these teams just changed everything?

Ted:

Well, first of all, a self-winding team in the CDL culture means that everybody on the team stands up for and values everyone else on the team. They also recognize the different problem-solving styles, interaction styles, and skill sets that are there, and they realize how to complement one another. Team members help one another out so that the overall team wins the game.

Secondly, they have very clear, negotiated service Careabouts with their colleagues and with their paying customers. And, they understand very clearly what the economic KPIs for their area of the organization are and how they affect the overall KPIs of the organization. They are informed. They're cooperative, and they also have developed a set of process-improvement and decision-making skills which allow them to take control of their processes without need for a lot of guidance. Self-winding teams know where their authority limits are, and so you let them take those skills, cooperation, and measurements and go for it within a clear authority zone.

Daniel:
Can you give us one example of a team who was just drowning when you got there and CDL elevated them to the next level?

Ted:
I'm reminded of a military logistics base in the United States. They coordinate supplies for all their military members all over the world. Suffice to say, they were not an entrepreneurial client-centered business. Their old habit was execute with whatever you've got on hand, good luck, and so on.

Basically, we were asked to come in (I was very honored to be asked) and see if we could help them implement that specific military branch's quality program. We were asked to bring our CDL cultural tools to achieve what the base was supposed to do but also make the task proactive, sustainable, voluntary, and enjoyable.

These folks showed up! We trained hundreds and hundreds of people week after week on CDL tools. They applied the tools, and they won their military branch's Quality Award. I received a civilian award from the commanding officer, which is one of the treasures of my professional life.

This is one example where bureaucracies became more like entrepreneurial business.

CHAPTER 6

PREPARING AND ASSESSING FOR CUSTOMER DRIVEN LEADERSHIP

So far, we've covered how Customer Driven Leadership works, and we've covered the components of CDL. In this section, I want to give an overview of what happens before you begin to implement Customer Driven Leadership.

The beauty of CDL is that it can be implemented in its entirety or in small, focused components. With the main goal of servant leadership and entrepreneurial problem solving remaining unchanged, the path you take to get there can be specifically catered to your needs. This chapter is designed to help you make an educated decision on your implementation process, one which will guide your organization to unprecedented success.

Then we will cover CDL assessments to help you understand how ready your organization is for CDL implementation. This will also cover what it means to be assessed as GREEN/YELLOW/RED and how to start from where you are.

Finally, we will cover some coaching, training, and speaking resources, and other team building tools you can use to improve your RED and YELLOW scores to make CDL implementation easier.

IMPLEMENTATION OPTIONS

The first thing we recommend is to begin to think about which CDL implementation route would best fit the needs of your organization:

Self-Implementation

- Leverages: CDL Implementation Guidebook(s).
- Advantage: it is very inexpensive
- Best for: small or flat organizations (a small number of teams / small hierarchy) and organizations with next to no budget for implementing.
- Recommended resource: (internally or externally) someone with project management and facilitation experience.

- Awareness: If the Organization overall is not GREEN, some organizational growth resources may be helpful first (Some Resources are included in the CDL Implementation Guidebook).

Guided Implementation

- Leverages: Internet course that supports CDL implementation, support calls, and CDL Implementation Guidebooks.
- Advantage: Videos guide your teams through the process; there are resources that can answer specific questions.
- Best for: moderate sized organizations (5-10 teams) and organizations with a moderate budget for implementing.
- Recommended resource: (internally or externally) someone with project management experience.
- Awareness: If the Organization overall is not GREEN, some organizational growth resources may be helpful first (our team can help you find additional resources to address specific needs, beyond the resources in the CDL Implementation Guidebook)

Work with CDL Implementer(s)

- o Leverages: A certified CDL implementer or implementer team will work with your organization to help you implement CDL guiding you through the process (an appropriate number of CDL Implementation Guidebooks will be included as well).

- Advantage: A professional or a team of professionals working together can guide you through the entire process significantly speeding up the process and helping to navigate around some organizationally unique pitfalls. CDL implementers are also specialists in specific industries and have deep coaching and training experience.

- Best for: well-resourced organizations of any size (price will scale based on the complexity of the organization).

- Recommended resource: No specific resources are needed. We will work with Human Resources or your internal Training Teams (as desired).

- Awareness: If the Organization overall is not GREEN, some organizational growth resources may be helpful first (our implementers can help you find additional resources to address specific needs, beyond the resources in the CDL Implementation Guidebook) .

CDL PRE-IMPLEMENTATION ASSESSMENTS

The second thing that we recommend that you do is take our free assessment online, and here is the website for that: CustomerDrivenLeadership.co/freeCDLassessment

This will give you a general idea of where your organization stands in its readiness for CDL implementation, but it is just a high-level, rough estimate based on the knowledge and visibility of the person filling out the survey.

At CustomerDrivenLeadership.co/CDLassessment we also have a relatively inexpensive paid full-version of the assessment tool that will assess the entire organization by:

1. Assessing each of your organization's teams, including:
   - The members of each team
   - The managers/leadership of each team
2. Providing a team-by-team mapping of readiness rating broken down into 7 key factors:
   - Support for Team
   - Support for Improvement
   - Support for Creativity
   - Commitment
   - Decision-Making
   - Improvement Tools
   - Team/Leadership Alignment
3. Rating every team as:
   - GREEN: GO—Ready for CDL implementation
   - YELLOW: PROCEED WITH CAUTION—Some areas of CDL could prove challenging, but options to improve readiness will be provided

- **RED: STOP UNTIL MORE PREPARED** - There are enough challenges that teams that are in the RED should begin working on some core improvements, working their way to YELLOW before implementing

4. Providing specific types of training/coaching/resources/materials that can help improve each team (as needed) based on its scores (we will endorse what we know; there are many other options that can improve each category), and additionally, the appendix of the CDL Implementation Guidebook will have specific resources that can also help.

5. The Organization will also be assigned a GREEN, YELLOW, or RED Rating that should be a good indicator in how ready it is for full implementation, partial implementation, or options to improve key areas to increase its readiness to implement CDL. Remember it is possible to begin CDL implementation in some areas before others in an organization.

CDL ASSESSMENT RESULTS

If you are GREEN at an Organizational-level, that means that you are 75% GREEN on average, and you have no RED scores. Your organization should confidently be able to engage in implementing CDL following whichever implementation strategy you have chosen. We consider a CDL Organizational Score of GREEN to be exceptional and a strong indicator that you are ready to embrace CDL implementation. GREEN means GO—Ready to Implement. You will still benefit greatly by working to improve where your organization has YELLOW individual scores while moving forward.

If you are YELLOW at an Organizational-level, that means that you are on average YELLOW and less than 25% of your scores are RED, OR you are on average GREEN but you have one or more RED scores. This is an indicator that you should start working to improve your RED scores as you plan for your implementation (this can happen concurrently). It is also a good idea to work to improve the areas where you are YELLOW, but you can do that as you implement with resources and suggestions provided below (there are additional resources in the CDL Implementation Guidebook). We consider a CDL Organizational Score of YELLOW to be equipped to proceed, but with an understanding that some key areas are going to need to be improved before CDL is fully implemented and fully productive. YELLOW means PROCEED WITH CAUTION.

If you are RED at an Organizational-level, it is an indicator that at least some of the areas of the organization might not be ready for CDL implementation at this time. The good news is our CDL Certified Implementers and partners know how to grow your organizational readiness. Our assessment will give you recommended suggestions of the types of training, coaching, tools, etc. that can help you grow where you need it most. This type of support is affordable and can be accomplished in a variety of ways in the section below (there are additional resources in the CDL Implementation Guidebook). We have found that a CDL Organizational Score of RED indicates that some pre-implementation growth should take place before engaging in CDL. It does not mean you have to wait, but it is a strong indicator that much of the organization is not going to be ready to embrace CDL. If some of the teams are YELLOW or GREEN, they can begin to implement CDL while leadership addresses specific RED scores across the rest of the organization. If you want to create the fastest car in the world and you built the world's best engine, putting that engine into a rusted-out chassis of a 1972 AMC Gremlin is going to be a really dangerous experiment. When it comes to CDL implementation, the organization needs to be strong, flexible, collaborative, and led by empowering leaders. Strapping an ACME rocket on your organization and lighting the fuse is not a recipe for success. Ready the organization first, then supercharge it. RED means STOP UNTIL MORE PREPARED (and remember there are many ways that we can help and there are many resources beyond those recommended in this book).

HOW TO IMPROVE ASSESSMENT SCORES

Here are some of the solutions that can help your Organization/Teams improve:

- Internal Trainers (now that they know where and what kind of training is needed, they can do the training themselves by finding the right curriculum)

- External Trainers (Experts in specific areas of growth)
- Mentors (GREEN team leadership can work with your RED/YELLOW teams and leaders)
- Coaches (Internal or External)
- Speakers (Experts in Key Concepts)
- CDL Implementers (fully equipped to help you mature wherever you need help)
- Assessment Tools (DISC, EQ Test, Kolbe, StrengthsFinder, Working Genius, Enneagram, VIA Institute on Character Assessment, etc.)
- Team Book Studies (self-facilitated or with external support, this is more useful to improve YELLOW scores than for pulling scores out of the RED)

If you have no idea where to find resources, one of my strongest recommendations is to start with Maxwell Leadership Certified Teammembers, who have access to many of the Maxwell Leadership Resources that can improve servant leadership, communications, values-based growth, etc. This recommendation comes from being a proud member of the Maxwell Leadership Certified Team, knowing their commitment to being "people of value, who value people, and add value to people," and being aware that they have tens of thousands of amazing members globally. I also know many other trainers, speakers, coaches, and resources that can grow your teams where they need to improve.

BASIC RESOURCES TO IMPROVE SPECIFIC ASSESSMENT SCORES

Below are the 7 Factors that are critical to successful CDL Implementation. Focus on getting the RED scores to at least YELLOW before proceeding, and then when implementing CDL continue to work the YELLOW scores up to GREEN. Here are some resources that can help improve each of the 7 factors:

1. Support for Team—*How to be a REAL Success* (John Maxwell), *Everyone Communicates Few Connect* (John Maxwell), *Change Your World* (John Maxwell), DISC, Kolbe, Working Genius, EQ, Diversity and Inclusion Training, John Maxwell Leadership Game, *Developing the Leaders Around You* (John Maxwell), *Good Leaders Ask Great Questions* (John Maxwell), *Leadershift* (John Maxwell)

2. Support for Improvement - *The 15 Invaluable Laws of Growth* (John Maxwell), *Sometimes you Win Sometimes you Learn* (John Maxwell), *How Successful People Think* (John Maxwell)

3. Support for Creativity—*Intentional Living* (John Maxwell), John Maxwell Leadership Game, *Good Leaders Ask Great Questions* (John Maxwell), *How Successful People Think* (John Maxwell), *Dream Big* (Bob Goff), *Think Again* (Adam Grant)

4. Commitment—*Put Your Dream to the Test* (John Maxwell), *Today Matters* (John Maxwell), *Intentional Living* (John Maxwell), *Atomic Habits* (James Clear)

5. Decision-Making—*Cultivate Courage* (Dave Cornell), *Put Your Dream to the Test* (John Maxwell), *Today Matters* (John Maxwell), *Intentional Living* (John Maxwell)

6. Improvement—*The 15 Invaluable Laws of Growth* (John Maxwell), *Sometimes you Win Sometimes you Learn* (John Maxwell), *Atomic Habits* (James Clear)

7. Team / Leadership Alignment (when Team and Manager scores are significantly unaligned)—*Becoming a Person of Influence* (John Maxwell), *Leadership Gold* (John Maxwell), *Developing the Leader Within You 2.0* (John Maxwell), John Maxwell Leadership Game, *The 21 Irrefutable Laws of Leadership* (John Maxwell), *Good Leaders Ask Great Questions* (John Maxwell), *Leadershift* (John Maxwell), *Leaders Eat Last* (Simon Sinek)

Once you have your scores YELLOW or better, you can begin implementation (while continuing to strengthen your teams through additional training). The CDL Implementation Guidebook will have additional tools that can support positive growth toward being GREEN and being fully ready for CDL. The next chapter provides a step-by-step overview of how to accomplish a successful CDL roll out in your organization.

CONVERSATIONS WITH TED ANDERS

Daniel:
If a company is not totally ready for CDL, what can they do to get themselves ready?

Ted:
Well, there are preparation tools that an organization can and really must apply, in order to begin allowing their employees to learn how to run the business and to trust them with it. A great place to start is with our CDL materials, with this book, and with the CDL Implementation Guidebook. We have the assessment instruments on the six health factors of an organization, exploring an organization's readiness to do Customer Driven Leadership. There are assessments for management and for staff to reflect on these six readiness factors, which involves such things as willingness to innovate, democratic decision making, quality process control tools in place, and so forth.

If they assess themselves and they fall into what we call the RED, this signals *Okay, you folks do not have the cultural positive tools and actual operation tools in place to become a CDL self-winding team and organization; however, you can, but you need to do these activities in the RED to get ready.* Once you've done those, you'll be ready to move towards the YELLOW (proceed with caution). Now, you can start some of the monthly CDL habits, but you're going to need to continue to learn these process control communication and decision-making tools in the YELLOW. Once those are done, companies can then move into very independent, self-directed, data-driven operation in, what we would call, an entrepreneurial GREEN.

Daniel:
Can you talk about some of the key indicators that somebody might be in RED?

Ted:
Here are six readiness factors:

1. Does the ownership/senior leadership really support strong teams? Do they really want strong subject matter teams to take responsibility and lead flow, or do they just call them teams because it sounds nice to have team members rather than employees? It has to be authentic. Leaders have to know how to build, coach, and motivate teams.

2. Is there really a genuine, authentic welcoming by owners and managers for improvement recommendations coming from the ranks; is that your workplace culture? Do people feel comfortable being able to stand up and say, *You know, something's wrong. This, this process or this division or this element doesn't work. And can we improve it?* Or are they smashed down for exposing error and waste and inefficiencies in the organization?

3. Does your organization celebrate support for innovation and creativity? I use those terms innovation and creativity intentionally separately. A lot of people use them interchangeably, but there is, in fact, a difference. Innovation is a subset of creative thought. Innovation means creating something novel or new. There's also elaboration, meaning adding detail to something that exists. It's not necessarily innovative, but it's better with the detail. Are they welcoming ideas for possibilities for the organizational feature? That's called fluency of ideas, which is an element of creativity. Are they looking for flexibility of thinking, people who see things from different perspectives?

4. Is there a sense of commitment to the organizational mission and vision? Is there a commitment to one another's best interests, which seem to be a real genuine aspect of the culture?

5. Does there tend to be support from the organizational leadership for decision making made by employees and frontliners? Certainly, if they have decision-making tools in place, that signifies a readiness factor. Do people at the organization know how to use problem-solving, decision-making tools together?

6. Is the organization trained and supported to use process-improvement tools? Do they understand ISO tools? Do they understand quality management tools?

Those are six really important readiness factors. If an organization scores low on three or four of those, they're not really ready. They're going to be in the RED and they need to get those tools in place to move forward.

Daniel:
I can see there could be a major disconnect between Management Scores and Team Scores. Might that be a seventh factor worth tracking? If Management Scores indicate we are GREEN across the board and the Team Scores are RED, you might be worse off than a YELLOW average. I could see that as a strong indicator that the team could use some training to communicate better and to better understand each others' perspectives.

Ted:
Yes. I can absolutely see the value in that.

Author's Note: this is how Ted's initial six CDL readiness factors became seven. I have worked with organizations where there was a major disconnect between team members and leadership and have used tools, like the John Maxwell Leadership Game and other types of training to improve communications and create a more cohesive perspective on the team.

Daniel:
If the Readiness Factors are indicators that a company has some experience with looking hard at itself and encouraging input, there has to be some basic understanding of how to use the types of tools that CDL is going to require to keep them on point. They need to understand the necessity of moving

toward serving their customers and optimizing how they do that. They need to see the inherent potential of transforming to whatever possibility the future holds. They need to believe that embracing CDL basically takes them out of the competition zone and makes them an industry leader.

Ted:
Exactly! Very well said! In addition to that core set of readiness factors, there are some others we can talk about, which may seem a little more subjective. One of the preparation tools we can offer is a normed instrument we created a couple of decades ago called The Social Diversity Sensitivity Survey. An organization can take the survey to determine their lifetime exposure to diversity and their actual value for diversity. These are important things to take a look at. For example, if there's no real value for diversity, there's going to be weak links in relationships, a lack of volunteerism, and so forth. This is an issue, especially in today's society.

I would also ask if leaders/managers see themselves as development coaches? There's a big difference between a manager and a coach, which is why even a sports team has a different name for the coach and the manager. Leaders should be asking if they have the skills or even the interest in coaching people towards better performance, or do they just want to hire and fire?

Daniel:
Leaders that cannot or do not want to coach can always look for outside support to empower their teams. What other solutions have you created to help move companies from RED to YELLOW to GREEN?

Ted:
We have put entire sets of actions in place which are required to grow management, teams, or employees who are not yet self-directed, self-measuring, and self-winding. We want teams that actually act like small entrepreneurial units and run themselves as an entrepreneurial business.

CHAPTER 7
CUSTOMER DRIVEN LEADERSHIP IMPLEMENTATION OVERVIEW

After you have done your CDL Organizational Readiness Assessment and have addressed the critical areas (those that were RED), you are ready to begin implementing CDL. Just a reminder there will be challenges ahead, but even as you move through those during CDL implementation, you will begin to see three big payoffs.

IMPLEMENTING CDL OFFERS THREE BIG PAYOFFS DURING IMPLEMENTATION

1. **For those who work in the organization** - Generally, within three months you will notice an increased

internal satisfaction, as well as improved relationships and process efficiency.

2. **For customers** - Within six months, you will likely see an increase in customer satisfaction and long-term loyalty.

3. **For the organization** - Within nine months, you can expect to see improved Key Performance Indicators.

I hope you will agree that those payoffs are exciting and have the potential to increase your organization's success and improve its culture. This chapter is intended to be practical and is aimed to provide an overview of *how* you might choose to roll out CDL processes within your organization.

While you will need to consider the various needs of your organization, CDL implementation can be introduced in seven steps:

1. **Form the CDL Guidance Team** - Secure Executive buy-in and commitment

2. **Geometrics of CDL** - Identify your organization's Geometrics of CDL

3. **CDL Implementation Core Tasks** - 5 Core Task Teams gather critical information needed for successful implementation

4. **CDL Power Orientation Seminar** - Orient the Organization

5. **Implement CDL (Phase 1)** - Roll out CDL fully or partially

6. **Conduct Three Practices Months of CDL** - Collect critical data

7. **Review Three Months of Data and Adapt** - Make needed adjustments and begin incentives

LOGISTICS OF IMPLEMENTATION

You're ready to begin implementing CDL processes, but where to start? The wonderful thing about CDL is its inherent flexibility. If the idea of overhauling your organization in terms of structure and culture causes an overwhelming feeling of anxiety, simply focus on a few of the most important aspects you'd like to try. Where would you like to see your biggest return of investment? What piece of this do you need badly enough to risk disruption? If you can't go all in, what can you take which will improve the future of your organization?

We know that growing pains are inevitable and that everything worth having is worth fighting for. Remember, an organization that cannot adapt and grow is a dying organization. The bigger the changes, the larger the potential for growth. This will take time and effort. We have found with CDL the time and effort you invest will be worth it, exponentially.

To help ease your impending anxiety, this is what a sample six month roll-out plan can look like, which you can reference and use as an anchor when imagining implementation at your organization. The more GREEN you are, the faster you should be able to roll out CDL, and the YELLOW and RED scores are going to slow you down, as might the complexity and/or size of your organization. Some large organizations might choose to begin implementing CDL in a sub-group of their organization and then consider expanding it from there once it stabilizes and begins to deliver increased value.

CDL IMPLEMENTATION STEP 1: FORM THE CDL GUIDANCE TEAM

Forming the Guidance Team encompasses figuring out who are the best people in your organization to lead the implementation of CDL.

If the organization is small enough, the team can engage everyone. For a medium-sized organization, it could be a partnership—perhaps a leader and member from each of the teams to represent all the players in the value chain. In a large organization, the Guidance Team would probably be composed of executives working with project managers to implement CDL. While there is certainly flexibility in the composition of your Guidance Team, the key is ensuring the people who are providing the vision don't become disconnected from the process. The leaders need to be present so that they have their hand in what the organization is working to create. Effectively, all of the senior leadership needs to be aware of the end goal and the day-to-day logistics of success. Their input is essential and needs to be built into the Guidance Team.

CDL IMPLEMENTATION STEP 2: GEOMETRICS OF CDL

This part of the implementation process involves conducting a one to two day "Geometrics of CDL" preliminary design session in which the Guidance Team works to prepare the tasks listed below for CDL implementation. (In smaller organizations, this can be done in a half-day session, and the size of these teams will scale depending on how complicated the organization is. Completing the five tasks below will provide senior leadership focus and direction and prepare the organization for Step 3:

1. Clarify Your Vision Statement (Review and Update, if needed)
2. Clarify Your Values (Review and Update, if needed) Overview Geometrics of CDL
3. Define Your Global Customer Careabouts (for the entire organization)
4. Map Out Your Value Chain
5. Establish Core Task Teams

Clarify Your Vision Statement

If you already have a vision statement, great. Does it currently reflect the direction your organization wants to move forward in? If not, you don't have a vision statement that serves you. If you do not have a vision statement that serves you, the Guidance Team should collectively create one. The vision should not only encompass who they're trying to serve right now, but should also include aspirations to grow in new directions (your future should be bigger than your present state in some way that matters to you and those whom you aspire to serve).

For example, if an organization is currently only selling widgets, and that's all they're ever going to do, they can become the world's best widget maker and shipper. They can be the best widget company in the world, if that's all they care about, but if they want to get into widgets and gadgets, then they need to think on a higher level. Whatever they're designing, the products need to exceed the expectations of their customers, fully satisfying their Careabouts. So the vision needs to be as big as it needs to be.

Clarify Your Values

First of all, does the organization have values defined? If not, they should work to establish their values. John Maxwell and Rob Hoskins' book *Change Your World* has a chapter called "Experience the Value of Values," and it has a great list of values that you can leverage. There is also another really good resource at viacharacter.org, which provides a list of individual character strengths (values). A CDL implementer can also guide your team through their thinking process to create a values list which will be the anchor for your organization's internal and external interactions.

Define Your Global Customer Careabouts

What is the organization trying to deliver? While Customer Careabouts may feel very similar to the vision, it involves what the organization is actively doing to satisfy the customers. You want this to be the compass heading for the entire organization. Customer Careabouts will guide your organization's CDL evolution, which will inevitably experience some growing pains. Keeping in mind that it won't be a perfect process, if anybody says, *Hey, I was working to try to get us to our destination, and this is how what I did was in support of trying to reach our Customer Careabouts* then they should get a lot of grace. This whole process evolves by people taking risks, by bringing forth ideas to help improve this global Customer Careabout. Successes and setbacks are part of the journey, and there needs to be room to make mistakes.

Map Out Your Value Chain

You need to know your organizational chart—who serves whom. From the top of the organization (or in CDL world the bottom), who do you directly serve; who do they serve, etc. until you reach the external or end customer. Many teams might provide some value to one another. For example, a sales team might be served by the warehouse team by providing them instructions on what to send and how to send it. The warehouse team might serve the sales team by providing the feedback that an order has been shipped; therefore, they know a good is coming in. They've got some good communication going between them. The point is, it's not always a one-way service where Team X does something for Team Y. Sometimes X does something for Y and Y does something for X, etc. Also remember it is rarely as simple as A to B to C to D to E to F... HR and other support roles potentially serve the entire company.

Create Your Core Task Teams

Each Core Task Team needs to be well-informed on everything that the Guidance Team has established above. These Core Task Teams also need to be aware of the core Geometrics of CDL so that they can build out those pieces in Step 3. Understanding how do we establish the Playing Field for this team? How should we reward people for doing well? The Core Task Team leaders act as project managers for CDL implementation, making sure everything is getting done and that nothing is falling behind schedule.

The 5 CDL Implementation Core Task Teams are:

1. The Customer/Community Careabouts Team

2. The Playing Field Team

3. The Incentives Team

4. The Internal Communications Team

5. The CDL Implementation Tracking Team

CDL IMPLEMENTATION STEP 3: CDL IMPLEMENTATION CORE TASKS

During this step, the five CDL Core Task teams will spend approximately one month completing assignments in the following areas:

1. *The Customer/Community Careabouts Team*—determines external and internal customer careabouts (obtains co-workers' understanding and initial buy-in).

2. *The Playing Field Team*—clarifies the strategic, financial, and operational boundaries around the CDL Freedom Formula.

3. *The Incentives Team*—develops and authorizes the cash and non-cash positive consequences to be provided based on monthly scores.

4. *The Internal Communications Team*—develops internal memos, e-mails, briefings, and other activities to ensure that the Customer Driven Leadership's technique is clear to all employees.

5. The *CDL Implementation Tracking Team*—transfers the employee list, team structures, and Careabout measurements into a customized, measurement tracking program in your HR department. This CDL tracking program supports the self-winding monthly measurement and improvement cycle by facilitating each team's collection and interpretation of monthly scores from both internal and external customers. If you

like, you can simply use our sample CDL performance tracking chart Excel spreadsheets for a simple way to begin, available at CustomerDrivenLeadership.co/PerformanceTrackingChart. Use the charts in the CDL Implementation Guidebook or go to CustomerDrivenLeadership.co/TrackingTools to explore investing in our automated system.

The Customer/Community Careabouts Team - Within each team, there is a Community and Customer Careabout contingent to the internal and external servant leadership mindset. This team establishes the initial or draft Careabouts across the organization. Team members need to be asking:

- How does my team serve the team upstream in the Value Chain?
- What about downstream from my processes?
- What do I need from the downstream team?
- What do I need from the upstream team?
- How should individuals grade or evaluate each other within a team?
- How do I fit into the big picture of making sure that everything is delivered to our external customers with the highest level of customer care?

The Playing Field Team - We know each team's Playing Field clarifies the strategic financial and operational boundaries around the CDL Freedom Formula. It essentially defines what each team is allowed to do and what their governing or limiting factors are for being able to solve problems within their own team.

The Incentives Team - They develop and authorize cash and non-cash positive consequences to be provided based on monthly scores, and there are many, many ways to do that. Earlier in the book, we mentioned a leader who paid out a third of the bonus in one month, a third of it in the next month, and a third in the month after that. That was a good way for him to spread the bonuses throughout the year for people. It also helps mitigate somebody from getting a huge chunk of cash and then quitting. There are a variety of options for incentivization that we will explore in the CDL Implementation Guidebook. In some cases, cash incentives might not be the right types of incentives, and there are other ways to incentivize teams, especially if you're talking about nonprofits. But cash motivates many people, especially at for profit companies.

The Internal Communications Team – Whatever the incentive, the CDL Internal Communications Team needs to ensure the Customer Driven Leadership technique is clear to all employees. People need to know exactly how to achieve success. The power of CDL is that everybody knows the rules of the game and everybody can play within the rules of the game to enjoy their work life more. To that end, the Internal Communications Team needs to have a plan to communicate everything about CDL during the design and implementation phases within the organization, as well as building out the structure to communicate clearly once it is fully implemented.

The CDL Implementation Tracking Team – Finally, the CDL Implementation Tracking Team needs to transfer the employee list, team structures, and the Careabout measurements into a customized measurement tracking system. Essentially, they will be pulling all the metrics they need to be able to do the monthly assessments. Additionally, in preparation for Step 4, teams should begin to address any skills and/or processes which have been allocated into the YELLOW. One thing that leadership or this team might explore is our CustomerDrivenLeadership.co/TrackingTools to help streamline this work.

CDL IMPLEMENTATION STEP 4: CDL POWER ORIENTATION SEMINAR

This step initiates the rollout of CDL to the entire organization. It needs to include some training. Some of the pre-implementation training and coaching may have already started, especially for teams with YELLOW scores. Teams with RED scores should get to YELLOW before implementing. You want to set everyone up for success because the trust factor can be severely damaged if you try to force this before teams are ready.

Many organizations choose to conduct a one or two day CDL Power Orientation Seminar as a kick off to Step 4. Ideally, the seminar should provide a dynamic overview of Customer

Driven Leadership and an explanation of the Geometrics of CDL, as well as a reminder of why CDL is important. Everyone is going to benefit from these changes! You want to be very clear as to what everybody's accountable for and how people will be rewarded. The seminar should also include an opportunity to focus on personal development skills. Essentially, you are going to be rewarding people for improving their servant leadership and there are going to be new incentives rolled out throughout the entire organization. People will want clarity on what's coming.

The seminar can be run in a variety of ways. If it's a large organization, you might consider breaking it out section-by-section, with the executive leadership present in support of the implementer. Maybe you have five different executive teams that make up the entire organization. Each team provides a briefing on Customer Driven Leadership. Then, as teams have cross-serving processes, individual managers and leaders can explain the details wherever teams have to work across executive lanes.

Effectively, as you go through this entire process, you want everybody on the same page, fully understanding that CDL is coming. It's coming, and it's going to benefit them. It's going to benefit the organization. It's going to make you better than your competition. It's going to get you more customer focused. And everyone is going to start having a heck of a lot more fun at work.

CDL IMPLEMENTATION STEP 5: IMPLEMENT CDL (PHASE 1)

In this step, the organization will conduct departmental team-building sessions to finalize draft "Customer Driven Performance Assessment Charts" and "Employee Driven Performance Assessment Charts." To begin, the information for these charts comes from the Customer Careabouts Team. Each department uses High-Performance Teamwork techniques (more details on these in the CDL Implementation Guidebook) to develop the charts and to prepare for upcoming monthly process improvement activities. In small companies, these charts can be drafted for initial use by leaders in 4-5 hours and then modified and completed by staff during the one-day CDL Power Orientation Seminar.

These are the things they will be evaluated on. What does exceeding expectations look like for each Careabout? This is critical for CDL. It's not just about giving grades and incentives, but it's also looking at the data, tweaking expectations, and becoming better as you move forward. The investment in time now is going to pay dividends in the future. You want everybody to fully understand what they're being evaluated on, how they are being evaluated, and how this serves both them and the customer.

CDL IMPLEMENTATION STEP 6: CONDUCT THREE PRACTICES MONTHS OF CDL

Conduct three months of CDL—focused customer service.

Collect scores at the end of each month and conduct a "CDL Score and Process Review Meeting" for 60-90 minutes at the beginning of each month. Teams make process and relationship change decisions in the meetings and then adjust their work behavior accordingly. Often, a significant amount of work needs to be done to improve relationships, as well as processes, during this timeframe.

These months are "practice" months. Everyone is getting used to the CDL tools and fine-tuning their charts and teamwork techniques. Generally speaking, only non-cash incentives are used during this practice phase to encourage everyone to "stick with it". However, cash can be used if the organization is ready for it. It certainly can speed up the results if planned and implemented thoughtfully. If not, cash incentives can inhibit buy-in by skeptics.

Before moving on to Step 7, enter all required information into your CDL Master Records Program developed and hosted by your HR department, unless you prefer to continue to use the Excel spreadsheet sample provided, or a "paper and pencil" mode, an app you develop for that purpose, or our CustomerDrivenLeadership.co/TrackingTools.

During this step, those teams who have scores that are "YELLOW" should be receiving training, coaching, and mentoring. It's crucial they are exposed to new concepts which will help them grow out of YELLOW (or potentially even RED) for the areas where they are not GREEN.

Whether it's an entire team or an individual, it's important to remind everyone to keep growing and investing in their readiness for CDL.

CDL IMPLEMENTATION STEP 7: REVIEW THREE MONTHS OF DATA AND ADAPT

Step 7 is essentially a review of what you have done over the past three months of practice.

After the organization has completed one fiscal quarter of CDL and made recommendations and adjustments, you want to finalize or adjust the Playing Fields, Careabouts, and incentives. You want to ensure an equitable degree of improvement challenge exists across all teams, if possible, and institute cash incentives to offer significant innovation and risk taking. Beyond just what a person or team's score is, if somebody comes up with a really good idea, there should be a process in place for providing a reward for innovation—cash or other incentives.

Finally, it's important to conduct an overview once everything's up and running. There is opportunity to continue to tweak your processes after every monthly review based on what you learn from each month's scores. This is how you continually get better and better at serving the customer, expanding the customer base, engaging and serving each other, and improving processes. Once you've made it past Step 7 and you have CDL implemented in your organization, you can begin to just focus on fine tuning and building on the improvements that it brings.

Once CDL is in place, we have found that over the next year will come exceptional growth, increased employee loyalty, innovation, attentiveness to market trends, and elevation above your competition. We want to encourage you to share CDL Best Practices amongst your teams, learn from each other, coach each other. It's also possible to look towards other organizations which are leveraging CDL and engage in dialogue about innovative ways to serve customers through new capabilities created through dynamic collaboration. Once you exist in a competition free zone, high performing organizations across all industries can inspire and elevate each other by sharing ideas, leading innovation, and collaborating in new ways, and when everyone is focused on serving the customer in the way that is important to the customer, the world starts to become a better place.

CUSTOMER DRIVEN LEADERSHIP FINAL THOUGHTS

In closing, my advice to you is simple. Trust the method we have designed…it has been applied successfully in all fields of endeavor on five continents, quietly and privately, for more than 20 years. Support it by using all three parts of the CDL Freedom Formula. We have seen organizations get frustrated when they don't adhere to the method! For example, if you mistakenly or purposely avoid the core, central customer-oriented demands or any of the key profit-driving KPIs when you develop your "Careabouts" and KPI content, then you will be focusing on trivia—not the business growth drivers. You won't see the "bottom line" impact that is possible, or you won't see it as quickly.

Also, don't try to manipulate employees with meaningless, cheap, or uncertain incentives. It would be better to have only psychological positive consequences for success. However, it is proven that even small, guaranteed cash incentives, the payout of which is truly under the control of the performer, sustains the CDL entrepreneurial, servant leadership culture for years. If your employees can give you 10x growth, why wouldn't you want to reward them for that?

In addition, all departments and leaders must meet monthly, using High Performance Teamwork to make substantial process change and improvement decisions. These process changes must be encouraged by everyone on the team—and often coached into existence by leaders. It is essential that the improvement and change actions be planned to stay within "The Playing Field boundaries," and that is the responsibility of leadership to make sure that happens. Otherwise, a department could destabilize balanced, cooperative, growth efforts.

Finally, remember that the power of CDL is derived from unleashing the freedom to innovate and take planned action to grow the organization! Do everything you can to encourage these freedoms. Be diligent about wiping out the "Three Killer B's" of "Bureausis," Butt-kissing, and Back-stabbing. CDL rewards positive action for the good of the vision and within the values of the organization. If you start seeing the "Three Killer B's" then things are drifting away from core CDL concepts such as: data-driven, customer-focused, self-winding, entrepreneurial, servant leadership, etc.

An entrepreneurial, servant leadership approach requires each of us to achieve personal and team excellence in a spirit of Customer-Driven cooperation. It is essential that we build–not destroy…that we create more than we criticize… that we not be satisfied to play childish games in our own backyard, but we set our sights on achieving the universe of possibilities.

CONVERSATIONS WITH TED ANDERS

Daniel:
Where have you seen CDL breakdown in the implementation?

Ted:
I can think of a few examples where the leader simply was in compliance with the need for a positive quality culture and didn't really mean it. They didn't really have it in their heart (and their ego) to be a servant leader and lift up others for the greater good of all involved. Leaders like this generally refuse to go to the bottom of the inverted organizational chart for at least a couple of hours a day, put one's ego aside, and lift everybody up towards the paying customer.

When we talk about successful implementations that were going quite well, and would go back to that company several years later to find that CDL culture and tools were not actively in place, in virtually every case where that might be the scenario, it was because either success occurred and the company was sold or there were boardroom power games played by people who didn't necessarily have that core value system which CDL infuses. They eventually made their power moves among shareholders and others to take control, not really recognizing or caring that one of the major reasons why the company had become so profitable, stable, and enjoyable was because of the culture and the tools of CDL.

If an organization is going to do this CDL culture, they need to dedicate the 12 to 18 months that it takes to really have it running like a finely-tuned, self-winding machine. It's very wise (from a business viewpoint and very caring from a human viewpoint) to be sure that the people you bring in next—when the CEO wants to retire, or when someone top leadership changes - to explicitly state that a core piece of the success of the organization is this culture, and we need a CDL oriented leadership or management replacement person to be hired.

Daniel:
Can you give us an example of a team you worked with that was not GREEN in readiness but still moved forward with CDL implementation at an appropriate pace and what they gained from the experience of going through the process with you and your team?

Ted:
There is a large, multi-site retailer with lots of retail outlets, a central office and supply center. Basically, they had an established 40- or 50-year culture of very top-down directive. Employees stayed in their various functional areas, showing up to do their job politely with one another, but they wouldn't ever proactively challenge the owners. The lead managers would suggest things would be different or better. When there was a generational shift to succession planning from the original generation to the new generation of family owners (who were more alert about the need for an entrepreneurial, proactive culture), the organization didn't have any team structure or team tools to be able to assign authorities.

They thought of the people as either the managers or the employees. They didn't think of themselves as a multi-level team. Certainly, the employees did not see themselves as anything other than needing to come in and do their job. They were there to make sure they've provided to the customer what is available on the floor. But whenever there wasn't inventory, there was a problem because there would be a dispute between employees around who's supposed to be responsible when the warehouse was empty. It just never was cooperative and coordinated. The new generation of family owners were so frustrated because they were dealing with micro-problems all the time, with no proactive action from staff.

We had to start forming groups of people into teams. Then we transitioned them into high-performance teams and finally into entrepreneurial, high-performance teams. There's a gradation of reality. People can hire folks and say, *Okay, you're on Team A and Team B,* but most times, they're going to a group where people care about themselves. What makes a team is a group of people with a label and a stated common purpose. Still, that doesn't guarantee they know how to work together or intend to work on the benefit of everyone together.

We had to define some structure, some roles and some rules together. Then a high-performance team begins to put in some expert techniques and "plays," like a winning sports team does. You could have some folks who would make a great pitcher, others who would be an amazing catcher or shortstop. That doesn't mean I know how to be the shortstop, in any kind of an expert way. It means I am part of a unified team standing on the field with roles and rules. A high-performance team understands they collectively have some expert methods they can use together to win the game. The left fielder and second baseman would have some specific processes or methods they use to work well together. The pitcher and the catcher have some very specific things they do together, so forth and so on.

Teams begin to understand when their customers are dissatisfied. It requires all expertise working together to make them more satisfied. How do you fix processes together? How do you work with one another to make sure inventory is ordered well in advance, or that it's labeled correctly and on the shelves? How do you examine the excellence or lack thereof that you have?

Once teams have these tools, you can begin to say, *Now, how would you like to be able to run this piece of the organization as if it were your own business?* Teams would come up with new inventory ideas, new ways to put sales in place, and new ways to reach out to the customer and manage those relationships in ways they never felt comfortable doing before. Then, they're beginning to act like they own the business in an entrepreneurial, Customer-Driven fashion.

So that's what we did with that particular multi-site, retail group. Eventually, local sites could run themselves as though they were, in fact, owning the business. What began to happen was inventory was in the right place at the right time at the right price. Employees coordinated back and forth between the local offices and the headquarters offices and warehouses. These coordinated efforts were in place so all local sites could win their numbers from their customers.

Yeah, it took about six to nine months, but it happened because the whole CDL culture was in place—the monthly habits, the ownership, being willing to turn the organization upside down and serve their people with what those people needed in order to get high scores from the customers. By actually having the owners go, *Yes, I get it,* CDL will lift teams up by getting them clear on their processes and rewarding them with proportional cash results. More importantly, we care, and we want to hear your improvements. People built trust in the new CDL system. They began to realize, *Proportional consequences do come to us if we, in fact, use the tools together as teams to focus on one another and the paying customer.* Over time, they solidified the culture.

Daniel:
At what point in the process did they start doing the monthly scoring?

Ted:
We pushed it off, at first, because there was no way they were ready to be accountable or to feel safe in front of one another. So we took about three months, and often this is the case.

To begin, we usually recommend a two-day orientation of the whole organization geared towards getting ready to become a Customer Driven Leadership organization. You have a really fun, rich, detailed, active two days, orienting everybody to the self-assessments and the culture. You give a glimpse of what's going to come up over the year ahead and listen to their problems and challenges. Then, you go ahead and say, *"Okay folks, we're going to do this"*. And of course, the employees are in the background going, *"Yeah, yeah. We'll see whether or not this will last!"*

What happens is you give them the picture of what's going to happen, but they don't really believe it, and they don't understand how to do it yet. So, you say, *"For three months, let's just practice. Let's play with the CDL charts. Let's see what your customers care about. Let's see what your colleagues care about. Let's just practice gathering some data on two or three of their Careabouts and related processes, and let's come together and say, if this were really a score, if this were really a live game, what the outcomes would be."*

You get together and you shape their monthly meeting habits and their monthly score collection habits. You shape a mindset of a positive, healthy, non-recrimination review of low scores. The owners and the senior managers should come to those meetings. When they get a low score for their leadership, or lack thereof (which they will get), it's very important that they model only positive reactions to low scores. Everyone begins to understand that no one is here to criticize and the data is not being used to upset each other. It's simply an opportunity to reflect on how everyone can do better. That's modeled over three months, and the employees begin to realize, *Oh, we really are doing this*. The leadership, who have been receiving low scores, are changing their behavior, and the more the owners do it, the higher the buy-in from everyone else.

Daniel:

Thanks Ted. Appreciate you directly sharing your experience and providing additional value and context to our readers. I hope that CDL becomes a true legacy of change for thousands of global servant leaders ready to invest in empowering their employees and serving their customers like they have never been served before.

CONCLUSION

If you take anything away from this book, I hope it's this: The culture of your organization is absolutely paramount to your success. In this context, success has multiple layers.

- Customer satisfaction and loyalty
- Employee retention, satisfaction, innovation, and belonging
- Financial abundance
- Self-winding teams which have accountability and ownership, leaving leaders the time and energy to do what they do best—inspire, connect, and reward

When employees and customers feel unheard, unseen, and uncared for, the results are obvious in your financial bottom line and in the relationships decaying within the organization.

CDL offers a way forward.

This book has provided you with tangible ways to create a culture which is based in care and accountability. It is the path to success. CDL helps organizations run themselves and run themselves in a healthy way that serves their employees and, of course, their clients.

CDL is the tool you need to inspire servant leadership involving everyone along the entire Value Chain. It offers the systems to maximize your delivery and nurture a deep awareness of how well you are satisfying your clients. Yes, we realize that CDL requires a shift in mentality, as well as some reorganization. Yes, we understand this may involve some growing pains and effort within your organization. However, if you take a step back from your hesitation and look at the benefits you will reap, we firmly believe the investment is worth it, exponentially.

Organizations which adopt CDL processes have shown that they:

- Stay ahead of the competition.
- Have valuable dialogue with customers, ensuring they feel well served.
- Have employees who love coming to work.
- Create teams where everyone is aligned with a shared vision.
- Have employees who understand their roles in the Value Chain.
- Have teams who work cohesively, collaboratively, and understand the system of hand-offs.
- Promote an environment and culture of innovation.

- Have teams who positively respond to the monthly assessments which drive constant improvement.
- Open up problem solving to the entire brain capacity of the organization where everybody is valued.
- Cultivate greater awareness to address opportunities and potential problems as those unknown unknowns quickly become known through CDL metrics.

CDL is the operating system which makes a healthy organization healthier. Organizations which rely on having managers running teams that loosely coordinate together will never have the ability to compete with an organization operating together like a well-balanced, self-winding machine. CDL is the whole organization, with one vision, one purpose, serving the customers the way they want to be served, anticipating and moving with the markets, innovating and staying ahead of hiccups, and always being at the cutting edge of innovation. All this while valuing all employees and letting everyone contribute with their diverse, unique experiences, gifts, and talents.

Customer Driven Performance is the key to your organization's vision. Without satisfied customers, you have nothing. Therefore, it's essential to cultivate knowledge about your performance and the relationships you build with your customers. You need to ask yourself, *How are we doing? How are we serving the client? How are the client's needs changing? Are there any slowdowns in the "pipeline" from the senior leadership's vision all the way to best customer experience on the delivery side?*

Key Performance Indicators are the touchpoints which ensure your assessments work the way they are supposed to work, so that you're driving the organization down the road of success led by its values and its vision to serve the client.

What is measured matters. It is critical to get that right at the senior leadership level so that everyone is on the same page and assessing the most important functions of the organization, delivering excellence for the clients. It is important to reassess as well, not only how well the organization is running but in what direction. Leadership still has a critical function to play, including addressing their own shortcomings in the monthly assessments. You have to be willing to lead by example.

It is critical that you are not wasting time tracking the things that don't really matter and you are focused on the things which will push you ahead of the competition and that will grow your organization according to its vision. When your teams become self-winding, that lets you, as the leader, solve the big problems, like *What comes next? Where can we expand? Who else can we work with? How to evolve new processes and new procedures that will even better serve our clients? Where else can we grow clients?* When you aren't trapped in the day-to-day management of your company, your energies can be spent looking at the future and imagining the possibilities.

If you want to undertake a monumental change in your organization's culture, or even a small shift to begin, we are here to support you. We offer several paths for you to follow to make sure you have a successful implementation.

- Start by taking a look at our website, which will help you assess your readiness to begin implementation of CDL.
  - CustomerDrivenLeadership.co/freeCDLassessment (Free high-level assessment)
  - CustomerDrivenLeadership.co/CDLassessment (paid full organizational assessment)
- Using the high-level overview provided in this book, you now have the capabilities to self-implement CDL basics in your organization.
- CustomerDrivenLeadership.co/TrackingTools is an app that is customizable to your organization's Careabouts, and that app feeds into a website where you will be able to track the outcomes of the assessments and take actions where you need to. This is not required, but it will allow you to export data to our team should you need help (sharing data is completely optional). No matter how you decide to implement CDL, you will have the tools to build out your own process for assessing should you not want to use our app/tool.
- If you have a smaller organization and are good at implementing new processes, you can do some

from the CDL Implementation Guidebook. It will also have the pre-implementation assessments (as mentioned above) and all the tools you need to map out your Value Chain and develop your Careabouts for each team.

- Ted and I have a full training program that will supplement the CDL Implementation Guidebook, and we will guide you through structured video lessons for each section of CDL implementation. We will have FAQs and resources to make sure that your questions get answered.

- You can hire a certified CDL implementer. They will be vetted, and we can help match you with the right coach or coaches to help your organization embrace CDL. Ted and I will be fully supporting our coaches to make sure that they have the answers they need to get you where you need to go with CDL.

I believe CDL can take you beyond where you think is possible, while creating a dynamic and empowering work environment and a team that will want to grow with you. I believe you will be more in tune with your customers and so far ahead of your competition that they will cease to be competition. Your values will begin to resonate beyond the walls of your buildings and start to positively impact your communities and the world. As Bret Weinstein and Heather Heying discuss in their book *A Hunter Gatherer's Guide to the 21st Century*, we live in a world of hyper-novelty, and it will take visionary leaders sitting around intellectual campfires coming together

Conclusion

to solve global problems, and few will have time to solve global problems, or even see them coming, if they are spending all their vision and energy just trying to keep their organizations surviving. The world needs better than that.

Ted and I hope that you give CDL a try, or work toward giving it a try (we will help with the tools on our website). We want to see the creativity of entire organizations working toward revolutionary solutions to global problems while empowering and invigorating the spiritual creativity and spark within those who contribute to its success. We are here to support your journey and wish you well.

Daniel Hammond and Dr. Ted Anders

EPILOGUE

A founding tenant of CDL is that we're essentially incentivizing people to be virtuous. We're asking our teams to care about themselves, each other, the customer, and the fate of the organization.

When people start to be virtuous, for whatever reason, it creates patterns. It's like when you have gratitude in your heart, your life can't help but be better. As bad as life gets, if you are grateful, there is always something to celebrate. We can cultivate specific patterns which shape our organization's culture to create an environment where people thrive. The seeds of this culture must be planted at the highest levels, within the leadership teams.

What does virtue look like?

It's knowing your people—knowing what they care about, where they fit, and what they aspire to be.

It's great leaders who are willing to say "*You are too good for the position that you have, but I don't have space for you to grow right now. Let me call some of my colleagues and find a place where you can really rise to your fullest potential".*

It's paying people what they are worth and sending the message, *I value the work that you're contributing to the organization and to our collective success.*

It's inviting employees to have a stake in the success of the company, in sharing a vision.

It's caring about and noticing hidden talent in your organization.

If we are asking people to be virtuous, then we need to see them as human and not just a cog in the wheel, and we need to acknowledge their innovation and pay them fairly.

CDL won't work without everyone in the Value Chain sharing vision and values. Similar to the way that the St. Louis Arch was built starting at both sides. If it's one fraction of 1% off, you fail to create a work of wonder.

Before working with the John Maxwell team, before being exposed to the principles of Dan Sullivan, I wouldn't have understood the value of CDL. I wouldn't have fully seen it for the depth of genius that it is.

When I first ventured out building my business, I was trying to sell a product that few understood. Even though I knew the value the product could deliver, I did not take the time to grow authentic relationships, and I was not sufficiently attuned to the needs of the clients that I was pursuing nor to the customers that they served. I didn't know about their Careabouts. I also didn't have a team, because I did not understand the value of having a team who could harness their collective genius to achieve a shared goal.

As I write this book, I am still a single person consultancy, but I have a team of over 100 gifted, brilliantly skilled people in my "Who" network. I have also had massive spiritual growth through inner healing and studying those wiser than I am. The things I used to chase now flow to me naturally. Ted and I, with help from our amazing team, built the Nightingale Nursing School facility with a lot of support from very generous organizations. Despite working together for over five years, Ted and I had not seen each others' Unique Abilities or zones of genius yet. When we saw each other in our unique giftedness, possibilities exploded. I wanted to know the depth and breadth of what Ted did because I saw it was very good. Ted walked me through his programs, and they are all amazing, but when he showed me Customer Driven Leadership, the genius within me leapt when it was exposed to Ted's genius of CDL (and all of the amazing partners he worked with to create it). I instantly wanted to share CDL with the world, and Ted must have also seen the potential because he asked me to co-author this edition before I could even identify the right way to ask to partner with him.

CDL is a shift in mindset as much as it is a shift in processes and systems. When run correctly, it maximizes every opportunity to exceed your organizational goals. I believe it can be implemented incorrectly, I believe it could be leveraged in unhealthy ways, but I don't believe it can fail if you are responding to the map it creates for your success. Maybe CDL cannot stop the Titanic from sinking once it breaks open on the iceberg, but it probably could have navigated around that iceberg had you invested in the tools to spot it earlier.

There are countless organizations around the world who are stunted by "the emperor has no clothes" syndrome—that people are either too afraid to speak up or they just don't care because it isn't their problem. The world's leading film maker Eastman Kodak invented the digital camera, but they completely missed the world changing technology because it didn't fit their current business model (stock price in February 2022, under $5 per share, although still with $1 billion in revenue in 2020). Apple, on the other hand, spends millions of dollars anticipating what people will want next (stock price in February 2022, about $165 per share, and $365 billion in revenue in 2021).

The Value Chain is like a pipeline that carries success to your clients. By doing the monthly assessments, you measure where things are not going, as well as possible, and you have a business health-based heat map of scores in every section of the pipeline. You don't have to watch for months to discover something is off and then deal with the section that touches the problem, only to find the problem didn't originate there. CDL helps you become laser focused and gives you the ability to see an issue almost instantly. It then provides tools to bring the whole team together to solve the problem with efficiency.

epilogue

Therein lies the genius! CDL creates incentives and metrics which take you where you want to go while making sure that people are doing the right thing. The system shows appreciation along the way with incentives which remind people, *Hey, good job for doing the right thing.* CDL is predicated on rewarding virtuous behavior.

CDL highlights your people's innate giftedness, and in return, those empowered people start doing the hard work of running the organization for you. They are greenlighted to manage problems, drive innovation, and find improvements within their zones of responsibility. Additionally, the connections between teams are strengthened so expectations and collaborations for success are better understood. CDL allows your organization to stay ahead of those you used to compete with and gives you the confidence that your clients are being well served.

By truly sharing your organization's vision and values and then asking people to be virtuous—to do their best and do the right thing—everyone wins, and *that's* the core message of this book and the lens I hope you see it through.

GLOSSARY

CDL Freedom Formula: Dr. Ted Anders' 3-part formula includes Customer Driven Performance Assessment, incentives and high-performance teamwork.

Community Careabouts: Focus areas for monthly peer assessment and data collection based on the virtues of caring for team members and adding value to the team. (How well does one contribute to the overall success of the team?)

Customer Careabouts: Focus areas for monthly data collection based on the needs of internal and external customers. (What do your customers actually need, want and care about?)

Customer Driven Performance Assessment: The process of monthly data collection based on Customer Careabouts.

Customer Driven Leadership Monthly Score Charts: These charts compile monthly data collection based on Customer Careabouts and will help you isolate areas for future improvement as well as recognize growth on previous focus areas.

Geometrics: Factors which influence the success of CDL, including the CDL Freedom Formula, Playing Fields, and personal/team power.

High-Performance Teamwork: Specific rules and roles to maximize the effectiveness of important meetings.

Key Performance Indicators (KPIs): Economic "health" factors which are usually tracked by accounting departments: return on investment, return on assets, gross profit margin, productivity etc.

Playing Fields: The basic limitations and boundaries which affect each team's autonomy, power, and responsibility: organizational plans, values, process constraints, budget, legalities etc.

Servant Leadership: Leaders lifting up everyone by doing the most good they can for others—so all can achieve their best and most satisfying potential for themselves and the team.

Value Chain: The backbone of the organization which determines the chain of action and decision making. Usually has a particular order and each component must link efficiently and effectively to add value to the final output (product or service) following along the organizational chart.

ACKNOWLEDGEMENTS

DANIEL WOULD LIKE TO THANK:

Carolina Batres, my wife, my perfect partner, and a "force of nature" in entrepreneurship.

Alex Hammond and Maria Gabriela Vitanza Batres Sabillon, my amazing kids who inspire me to be the best I can be.

Dianne Hammond, PhD, my mom who taught me to challenge what's possible and seek the Truth above all things.

Jim Hammond, my dad who taught me to love and value everyone, how God should always come first, and to do things the "right" way.

Kathryn Hammond, my little sister that in her all too short life instilled in me a love for serving and Honduras.

For my partners in the LoveLight Campaign for Central America, thank you for serving a cause so big it could change the world and millions of lives for the good.

For the rest of my incredibly loving family; superstar aunts, uncles, and cousins.

For all of my in-laws, especial Mario Batres and Blanca Cervantes, what an extraordinary family to be part of.

For Greg Oliver, and the rest of the Christ Restoration Center Ministries team for letting me serve with them and serve others.

For all my dear friends, but especially Dave Cornell and Debora Swartz for how they make the world better and this book too.

For my authentic friends in BIP100 and ECI.

For Dan Sullivan and Strategic Coach and John Maxwell and Maxwell Leadership for growing me into a Free Frontier Focused Transformational Servant Leader.

For everyone who has shared their unique gifts with me and the world.

TED WOULD LIKE TO THANK:

Beverly Fisher, who has been a consulting colleague through every step of CDL development, application, and maturation. She is one of the top leaders in team building, leadership building, and organizational performance assessment. Thank you for being a mentor and colleague for more than 30 years.

The generations who came before me—health care professionals, education professionals, and medical professionals—who have worked in their communities to ensure decisions are made with heart and soul for the best outcome for us all.

My great grandparents, my grandparents, and my parents.

The excellent professors I had at Furman University, who pushed me towards excellence when I didn't necessarily want to commit to it.

Wilson Harrell, who was a butt-kicking mentor in entrepreneurship, who helped me find value my entrepreneurial self and my mindset. What he taught me has been extremely valuable.

All of the original CDL consultant team, who were always ready to go around the world to prove this strategy.

Thomas for being one of the first major implementers and who has stuck with CDL for more than a quarter of a century. His major success has lifted up the lives of hundreds of families because of his dedication to the values and technique of CDL. He's been a model and a lighthouse for other companies who wish to learn, and his willingness to do so is so valuable.

To my clients, many of whom have become lifelong friends.

ABOUT THE AUTHORS

Daniel Hammond lives in League City, TX, is an entrepreneur, and serves in the senior leadership of the LoveLight Campaign for Central America working to solve root causes of irregular migration in Honduras, El Salvador, and Guatemala. He is a U.S. Army combat veteran, paratrooper, expert interrogation instructor, and course developer. He is one of the best Cyber Exercise consultants in the world, an expert in scenario design, and a Cyber Security evangelist. Daniel collaborates with others, especially entrepreneurs, to achieve new capabilities maximizing their areas of genius. He has worked with cabinet-level officials in four countries in four different roles.

Dr. Ted Anders is an experienced founder with a demonstrated history of working and providing leading innovations in the management consulting industry. Skilled in building sustainable, highly profitable, customer-centric cultures in both For-Profit and Non-Profit Environments, Leadership & Team Coaching, Innovation, Public Relations,

Entrepreneurship, and Team Building. Strong business development professional and humanitarian, social justice leader with a BA, MA, Specialist Certification, and PhD focused in Educational Psychology from Furman University and University of Georgia.

Printed in Great Britain
by Amazon

85572075R00109